QE2 Deck Plans.

Deck Signal

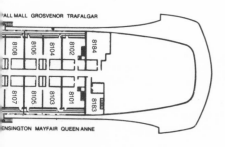

PALL MALL GROSVENOR TRAFALGAR

KENSINGTON MAYFAIR QUEEN ANNE

Deck Sports

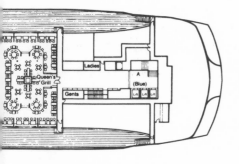

Boat Deck

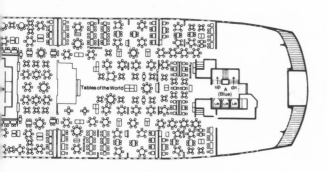

Upper Deck

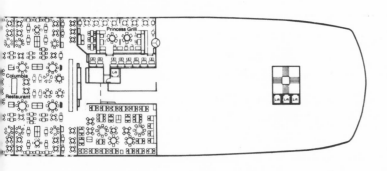

Quarter Deck

(Continued on back)

Q E 2

Ronald W. Warwick

William H. Flayhart III

Q E 2

W.W. NORTON & COMPANY

NEW YORK · LONDON

The text of this book is composed in Gill Sans,
with display type set in Gill Sans Bold and
Garamond Italic. Composition by Trufont Typographers.
Manufacturing by The Murray Printing Company.
Book design by Karen Salsgiver, Homans/Salsgiver.
Cover design by Mike McIver.

Published simultaneously in Canada by Penguin
Books Canada Ltd, 2801
John Street, Markham, Ontario L3R, 1B4.

Printed in Hong Kong by South China Printing Co.

First Edition

Library of Congress Cataloging in Publication Data

Warwick, Ronald W.   QE2.

   1. Queen Elizabeth 2
(Ship)   I. Flayhart, William H. III.   II. Title.
VM383.Q32F53   1985
387.2'432   84–14819

ISBN 0-393-01885-7

W. W. Norton & Company, Inc.,
500 Fifth Avenue, New York, N.Y. 10110

W. W. Norton & Company Ltd.,
37 Great Russell Street, London WC1B 3NU

1 2 3 4 5 6 7 8 9 0

CONTENTS

Dedication

The Cunard liner QUEEN ELIZABETH 2 was laid down just as the world entered a period of rapid technological development, and suffered some of the penalties of innovation. She was completed just as the era of the great North Atlantic passenger liners was coming to an end, beaten by the faster and cheaper liners of the air. Fortunately for her, she found a new career in cruising, although, at least in one respect, she followed the tradition of her predecessors by acting as a troopship. Among much other detailed information, this book describes her crucial part in the successful Falkland Islands campaign, which is likely to remain the most dramatic episode in an already very full career.

H.R.H. THE PRINCE PHILIP
Duke of Edinburgh

Foreword

Incessantly since 1958, following the introduction of jet service across the Atlantic, the media around the world has continuously marked the extinction of one great ocean liner after another. It is not surprising that many people in the world think the passenger ship business is "long dead." Shortly after QE2, the last of the great liners, was launched, experts reported that her life would be a short one. Thank God, QE2, and for that matter the cruise industry, is alive and well.

It is true that QE2 is the lone survivor of regularly scheduled transatlantic service by ship, and this service is only for a part of the year. Overall, including her transatlantic service, QE2 has become a destination all unto herself and, because of this, has also become a commercial success. Indeed, this book, THE QUEEN ELIZABETH 2, gives an understanding of why a person would want to sail in QE2. The book admirably captures the history and essence of this "City at Sea."

RALPH M. BAHNA
President and Managing Director
Cunard Line Limited

Acknowledgments

Any volume such as this involves substantial assistance from a broad selection of friends, acquaintances, and associates. Every effort has been made to use original material on the QE2 and previously unpublished photographs. The collections of the authors' were voluminous and involved nearly 5,000 pages of historical and descriptive information assembled over a period of some twenty years from the time the replacement of the original QUEENS was first discussed. Nevertheless, the final product would not have been possible without the unstinting aid of a great many individuals around the world.

The authors extend their grateful thanks to His Royal Highness Prince Philip, the Duke of Edinburgh, for graciously providing a dedication to this work on the QUEEN ELIZABETH 2 in recognition of the role she has played in British commerce and industry over the past twenty years since her keel laying in 1965.

The authors also wish to extend particular thanks to Ralph Bahna, president and managing director, Cunard Line, for agreeing to write a foreword to the work and for his generous support over the years.

A primary debt in the creation of this book must be acknowledged first to two ladies. Without the omnipresent support and constant editorial criticism

of Debbie Flayhart, gourmet cook, history major, and author, there would
have been no book within the schedule desired. Without the good-humored
arbitration capacities of Kathleen McDevitt, travel expert, lawyer, and author,
the book might not have made it through some difficult moments. To both
ladies go the thanks of both authors.

Of the first magnitude in importance also was the contribution of Alice
Marshall, director of public relations, Cunard Line, New York, who spent
hours reviewing the manuscript and offered many discerning comments. The
editorial work of N. R. P. Bonsor, dean of the world's maritime historians,
from his homes on Jersey, the Channel Islands, and Alicante, Spain, remains
matchless. No living soul can proof a manuscript in steam maritime history like
this vibrant octogenarian! Commodore William E. Warwick, C.B.E., R.D., R.N.R.,
reviewed the manuscript for authenticity in regard to the building of the liner
and her first years in commission. Captain Robert H. Arnott, R.D., R.N.R.,
master of the QUEEN ELIZABETH 2 and author of *Captain of the Queen*, read
sections of the manuscript and detected some points for consideration. First
Officer Philip Rentell also supplied valuable guidance on the Falklands experience. Other individuals who were helpful in many ways were Susan Alpert,
Patti Kostovitch, Leonard Karp, James Love, Dr. Eugene McNinch, Neil
Osborne, John Samardza, and Jeremy Townsend, assistant editor at W. W.
Norton, and Jack Marland, former chief engineer of QE2.

Photography for a work like this always commands a great deal of effort
and no small degree of luck—often in your selection of friends. The authors
wish to thank Malcolm Scanlan for many of the excellent photographs of the
QUEEN while in Her Majesty's Service and in the Falklands. A. C. Novelli
supplied a number of unique shots of the QUEEN ELIZABETH 2 during her
launching, and John H. Shaum Jr.'s photographs of the maiden arrival of the ship
in New York gave a special perspective on that event. David Barnicote's
photographs of the liner squeezing through the Panama Canal (shore shots)
were dramatic. It is impossible to thank sufficiently such distinguished and
generous maritime collectors and historians as Frank O. Braynard, Walter
Lord, John Maxtone-Graham, Peter T. Eisele, and Everett Viez for their help
and advice at moments of calm and of crisis. Additional photographs of scenes
on board the liner and on various cruises were taken by Debbie Flayhart,
Kevin Jones, Kathleen McDevitt, and James Machlachlan with the special
assistance of Claudia Blondeau, Vallerie Blondeau, and Nancy Brown. A substantial amount of aid was also given the authors by the Audio-Visual Center
of Delaware State College under the direction of Glenn Sturge, with Linda
Martin in charge of photography and Leon Gardner handling video-taping.

John Nicholson, the distinguished marine artist of Leeds, England, generously offered his original oil paintings of some of the great liners for inclusion
in the work. Jack Norman lent his fine philatelic collection featuring stamps of
the QUEEN.

At Delaware State College the authors wish to acknowledge the assistance of Dr. Luna I. Mishoe, president; Dr. James Lyons and Dr. H. R. Williams, successive vice-presidents of academic affairs; Dr. James Valle, chairman, Department of History and Political Science; Dr. Daniel Coons, director of the William C. Jason Library Learning Center; and Margaret Houchin (reference) and Helen Walker (circulation desk). The various members of the faculty research committee over the years have generously supported research in maritime history. Peggy Bingham and Dorothy Durham also helped in matters large and small at various times.

The authors also wish to thank the staffs of the following American institutions: Library of Congress, Prints and Photos Division; U.S. Department of the Navy, History Division and Naval Photographic Division; National Archives; University of Baltimore Library; Alderman Library of The University of Virginia; Libraries Division of the State of Delaware; Mystic Seaport; Peabody Museum; The Mariners Museum; The New York Public Library; The Museum of the City of New York; and last, but far from least, The University of Baltimore Library with the collection of the Steamship Historical Society of America (and the incomparable Laura Brown). The following British institutions also warrant special thanks: The British Library; The University of Liverpool Library; The Public Record Office; The Institute of Historical Research; National Maritime Museum; Imperial War Museum; and London House. Among maritime and naval societies the assistance over the years of the Society for Nautical Research, Steamship Historical Society of America, United States Naval Institute, and World Ship Society has been appreciated.

Finally, the authors would like to acknowledge the advice and support of Eleanor Woods, literary agent *sans pareil*, and James Mairs, vice-president and director of manufacturing, W. W. Norton & Company., without whose constant encouragement and understanding this work would not have been possible. Mairs is extraordinary in being an editor whose criticism one learns to appreciate and whose friendship one grows to respect. To a myriad other helpers we extend our grateful thanks.

Q E 2

CHAPTER ONE

*The British
and North American
Royal Mail
Steam Packet Company
(1840)*

The maritime heritage that gave birth to the QUEEN ELIZABETH 2 stretches back over a period of nearly a century and a half and involves a transatlantic experience from its inception. The men who conceived the spanning of the Western Ocean with a line of steamships came together from North America and Great Britain and began 150 years of international cooperation and strong commercial ties sustained by the Cunard Line and the other great North Atlantic lines.

The Industrial Revolution had progressed far enough by the 1830s to make the idea of transatlantic communication by means of a fleet of steamships plausible. The desire for dependable delivery of the mails on which imperial communication and commerce depended prompted the government of Her Majesty Queen Victoria to invite interested parties to tender for a contract. Samuel Cunard of Halifax, Nova Scotia, was the successful contender. His contract to deliver the mails across the Atlantic from Great Britain to North America was signed on May 4, 1839.

Samuel Cunard was a highly successful and enterprising Canadian businessman of Scottish ancestry and one of a group of twelve individuals who substantially directed the affairs of Nova Scotia. Cunard was largely unknown in Britain, although he was the agent of the East India Company in Halifax and was instrumental in establishing a thriving mail service between Halifax, Boston, and Bermuda. He also was one of the founders of the Quebec and Halifax Steam Navigation Company. Their steamer ROYAL WILLIAM had enjoyed one of the earliest successful crossings of the Atlantic in 1833. Cunard had the reputation for being not only a very astute businessman but also an individual endowed with exceptional diplomatic ability. He would need all the ability and charm he possessed to succeed!

In Halifax Cunard's breadth of vision in wanting to tender for the Admiralty contract went unappreciated. The reputation of the North Atlantic was too awesome and the steamship too novel for enough of his worthy associates to back him. Accordingly, in January 1839, Cunard sailed for Britain to pursue matters on his own. His willingness to cross the North Atlantic in a sailing ship in mid-winter demonstrated the intensity of his ambitions. He carried with him a letter of introduction from the governor-general of Nova Scotia, which may have helped him gain an interview with Charles Wood, the secretary to the Admiralty. Wood encouraged the Canadian entrepreneur to submit a formal bid.

The Cunard bid for the privilege of carrying the mails was handed to the Admiralty on February 11, 1839, and involved a commitment to provide three steamships of 800 tons and 300 horsepower each. A feeder service from Halifax to Quebec using a smaller vessel was envisaged, as well as one from Halifax to Boston, with the Canadian port being the western terminus of the North Atlantic service. Cunard felt that the contract should run for ten years at a compensation of £55,000 per year. The commitment on the part of Cunard was daring, since at the time of submitting the bid he had neither financial backers for the line nor a builder for the ships.

James C. Melvill, the Secretary of the East India Company in London, advised Cunard about who would be the best builder of the new ships. He recommended Robert Napier of the Scottish firm of Wood & Napier, who had built a number of steamships, including the very successful BERENICE for the East India Company. John Wood built the hulls, while Robert Napier was the engineering genius responsible for creating the engines. Napier and Cunard became business associates and close friends; their relationship lasted the rest of their lives. After Cunard's death in 1865, Napier commissioned a portrait of his friend to be given to Cunard's daughter Elizabeth. In acknowledging receipt of the painting, Elizabeth Cunard thanked Napier "for a gift that must be valuable to me for its own sake, as well as for the sake of the donor, whose name has been familiar to me from early childhood in connection with much I have heard of science and natural energy and talent."*

Cunard wrote to Napier for prices on the ships, and Napier quoted a price of £40 a ton. When Cunard met Napier in Glasgow, he admitted that the quotation was fair but, because he was ordering three identical vessels, he was willing to pay £30,000 per ship for the multiple contract. Napier agreed and Cunard got his ships for £37 a ton—a good Scottish bargain. What Samuel Cunard may not have known was that Napier had also contemplated transatlantic service as early as 1833 and had drawn plans for vessels of approximately the same size and power as the future Cunarders, but he had not been able to interest anyone in his proposals. At that time the idea of establishing a transatlantic steamship line had seemed as unreasonable as a flight to the moon. Less than a decade later the ships were being ordered.

Robert Napier fully realized that the success of the Cunard ships would be vested in their dependability. If they could depart and arrive on schedule time after time, then the public would patronize the vessels and they would earn their keep. Nothing else really mattered. Napier believed that the finest area of the world in which to observe steamship traffic was the Clyde and the highly competitive short sea route from Glasgow to Belfast. Accordingly, Napier became a familiar figure crossing back and forth on existing steamships, recording their characteristics and evaluating their performances. Out of these observations Napier concluded that the ships Samuel Cunard had ordered were too small and underpowered for dependable service on the North Atlantic. He took the figures to Cunard and the decision was reached to increase the size of the first ships from 800 to 960 tons, and their engines from 300 to 375 horsepower. Unfortunately the increase in size and horsepower added £2,000 per ship to the cost. In addition, Napier convinced Cunard that at least four ships were needed if year-round operations were to be maintained. The new expense was a hard blow to Cunard's plans, but Napier introduced him to three other Scots, James Donaldson, George Burns,

Samuel Cunard (1787–1865), a Scotsman who lived in Halifax, Nova Scotia, was the guiding force in 1840 behind the creation of the British and North American Royal Mail Steam Packet Company, which from the very beginning was known as the Cunard Line.

*Cunard Line, The Cunarders 1840–1969, A Transatlantic Story Spanning 129 Years, Cunard Line: London, 1969, p. 31.

and David MacIver, all of whom had important maritime interests on the Clyde and Liverpool and were willing to follow where Napier led. The result was the creation of the British and North American Royal Mail Steam Packet Company, which was founded with a capital of £270,000 acquired in a matter of days from thirty-two businessmen. George Burns' business acumen and good sense were so well known that he became the critical fund raiser, but Samuel Cunard put up the largest amount (£55,000) and the new line was familiarly known as the "Cunard Line" from its inception. The contract for the new ships was signed on March 18, 1839, and the creation of the enterprise was guaranteed.

One of the strengths of the company from its founding was sufficient capital to establish itself and to weather adversity. Its solid foundation permitted Napier to enlarge the size of the ships once again to 1,100 tons and 420 horsepower. At the same time Cunard returned to the Admiralty with the information on the ships and suggested that it would be an excellent postal and economic proposition if the vessels continued on to Boston from Halifax. A new contract was signed on July 4, 1839, with an increased subsidy of £60,000 for the enhanced service. The Admiralty agreed to Cunard having a biweekly service between March and October and only a monthly service in the winter months of November to February, when the cost in men and ships with little cargo or passengers would be too high. Napier's company was feverishly at work on the engines, but he had elected to subcontract for the hulls, and the first of these was launched by Robert Duncan of Greenock on February 5, 1840, as BRITANNIA.

The mail contract was supposed to take effect on June 4, 1840, but the fitting out and trials of the BRITANNIA took a little longer than expected and she was not ready to sail until July 4, 1840. A special Admiralty dispensation was allowed, fortunately, since the penalty for missing a sailing was £15,000,

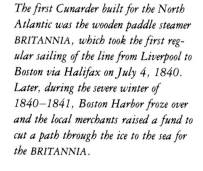

The first Cunarder built for the North Atlantic was the wooden paddle steamer BRITANNIA, which took the first regular sailing of the line from Liverpool to Boston via Halifax on July 4, 1840. Later, during the severe winter of 1840–1841, Boston Harbor froze over and the local merchants raised a fund to cut a path through the ice to the sea for the BRITANNIA.

one-fourth the annual subsidy. Under normal circumstances an unexcused delay of more than twelve hours resulted in a £500 forfeiture, although the Admiralty usually looked with a generous eye upon any mechanical failure or natural catastrophe.

The maiden sailing of the BRITANNIA captured the imagination of the Liverpool public, and she was given a rousing send-off, as commemorated by the famous painting of the occasion. At the time of her commissioning BRITANNIA was 1,135 tons, 207 feet in length, and 34 feet in breadth, with a service speed of 9 knots and accommodations for 115 individuals, as well as 225 tons of cargo. The BRITANNIA sailed with sixty-three brave passengers, including Samuel Cunard, and made the 2,534-mile crossing to Halifax in 12 days, 10 hours. She remained there a brief 8 hours before continuing on to Boston, which she reached in 46 hours, with a net steaming time of 14 days, 8 hours. Each morning at 6 AM while she was at sea, her engineers were instructed to "weigh up" 23 baskets of coal, with 50 pounds of the precious fuel per basket, and to watch the consumption carefully during the day in order to ensure that there would be enough left to reach Halifax or Boston. Coal was like gold to the new steamship line, costing 8 shillings ($10.00) a ton in Liverpool and 20 shillings ($25.00)* a ton in Boston. The projections were that the furnaces of the line's ships would consume 9,960 tons of coal a year.

The citizens of Boston gave the ship and her owner a hero's welcome. Contemporary accounts credit Samuel Cunard with receiving 1,873 invitations to dinner from delighted Bostonians. He also was presented with a large ornate silver vase suitably engraved with a commemorative inscription and a picture of the BRITANNIA that now graces the main entrance to the Columbia Restaurant on the QUEEN ELIZABETH 2.

The UNICORN, a 640-ton paddle steamer hitherto of the Burns Line between Glasgow and Liverpool, made her maiden voyage May 16, 1840—three months before the BRITANNIA. The UNICORN established the feeder service between Pictou and Quebec, although on this voyage she continued from Halifax to Boston with Cunard Line supplies. The BRITANNIA's own return crossing to Liverpool from Boston took only ten days, with the Gulf Stream and favorable winds to help (and, as a rule, most eastbound crossings were faster than westbound ones). The BRITANNIA was followed by the ACADIA (a poetic name for Nova Scotia), the CALEDONIA (Scotland), and the COLUMBIA (the United States), with the last of the four being in operation by January 5, 1841.

Cunard Line sailings were normally on the 4th and 19th days of each month (March–October), and on the 4th day during the winter (November–February). If the date fell on a Sunday, a Monday sailing was substituted. One-class fares were quoted at 34 guineas (£35.7, or $882.40) to Halifax and 38 guineas to Boston, initially with all food and wine included. After about

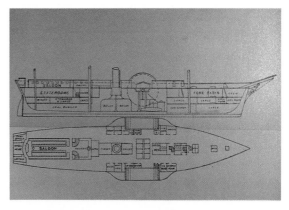

The deck plans of the BRITANNIA show the basic arrangement of a paddle steamer, with the machinery and paddle boxes occupying the center of the ship and the passenger areas fore and aft. The 1,135-ton ship, with a length of 207 feet and a breadth of 34 feet, could steam at 9 knots and transport 115 passengers and 225 tons of cargo.

*Throughout the text the monetary exchange rate is of that of the year concerned.

nine months it was stated in the company literature that all wines and liquor would be extra. Costs soon outran all estimates and the situation became quite serious. The partners put together a forthright explanation of their position for the Admiralty and, after due consideration, the subsidy was raised to £81,000 per year, but with the understanding that a fifth steamer would be built to ensure the continuity of service in the case of disaster. The HIBERNIA (named for Ireland) entered service on April 18, 1843, and proved herself a record breaker, crossing from Halifax to Liverpool in 9 days, 10 hours at 11.21 knots. The wisdom of the Admiralty's insistence on a fifth vessel was soon made dramatically clear when the COLUMBIA was wrecked in dense fog on Seal Island near Cape Sable. All passengers and crew miraculously were rescued and were transported to Halifax and Liverpool by the MARGARET, a paddle steamer that normally alternated with the UNICORN in the Canadian feeder service. The company did not even have to charter a replacement vessel and thus lose the fares of those who were saved by virtue of this stroke of luck. The Cunard line began to establish a reputation for safety that eventually gave it the proud record of not having lost, through the fault of the company, a single passenger at sea during peacetime in nearly 150 years. When news of the disaster to the COLUMBIA reached Liverpool, a replacement was promptly ordered and named CAMBRIA (for Wales).

Without the Admiralty subsidy, all the other British-flag North Atlantic passenger lines ceased to exist by 1846. Cunard was willing to extend operations to New York if an appropriate contract could be negotiated. This was achieved in 1847, when the subsidy for carrying the mails was increased to £156,000 in return for Cunard's commitment to maintain a weekly service during the period March–October and a biweekly sailing during the winter months. The feeder service from Pictou to Quebec never lived up to Cunard expectations and was withdrawn.

The HIBERNIA sailed from New York on January 1, 1848, thereby beginning Cunard's long association with that American port. Four new paddle steamers were ordered to maintain the new schedule, and they were substantially larger than the original ships of the fleet, with dimensions of 251 feet by 38 feet and a passenger capacity of 140. Napier again won the contract for the ships and built the engines while subcontracting the hulls. The first of the new steamers was the 1,826-ton AMERICA. Her sister ships were the NIAGARA, EUROPA, and CANADA, all completed in 1848. This brought the Cunard Line up to nine ships, six of which were sufficient to maintain the weekly service. Hence the first two ships, the BRITANNIA and the ACADIA, were sold to the German Confederation Navy. The BRITANNIA continued in service until she was sunk as a target vessel in 1880. Among the new vessels, the CANADA distinguished herself by an eastward passage of 8 days, 12 hours, 44 minutes from Halifax to Liverpool at an average speed of 12.41 knots.* The evolution

The great American competitor of Samuel Cunard in the 1850s was Edward Knight Collins (1802–1878), who founded the New York and Liverpool United States' Mail Steam Ship Company in 1850, which was universally known as the Collins Line.

*N. R. P. Bonsor, *North Atlantic Seaway*, Brookside Publications: Jersey, Channel Islands, 1975: 2nd ed. in five vol., V, p. 1876.

of communication on land by virtue of the invention and introduction of telegraph facilities meant that during the late 1840s and 1850s messages landed at Halifax were telegraphed ahead to Boston and reached major American metropolitan areas far ahead of the Cunarders themselves.

The guiding philosophy of the British and North American Royal Mail Steam Packet Company was conservatism. Under no circumstances would the Cunard Line tackle innovations or major advances in marine architecture or propulsion until the results were well established by other steamship lines. Upon occasion this placed the Cunard Line at a disadvantage when superior ships were brought into service by enterprising competitors, but the Cunard fleet also contained very few unsatisfactory ships during the nineteenth century and their safety record was unsurpassed by any competitor.

In the 1850s the great opponent of the Cunard Line was an American-flag concern, the New York & Liverpool United States' Mail Steam Ship Company, universally known as the "Collins Line" after its principal founder, Edward Knight Collins. This American venture was established with the goal of providing direct service from New York to Liverpool with larger, faster, and more luxurious vessels than Cunard. The first Collins steamers were named for the great bodies of water of the world and the 2,845-ton ATLANTIC (284 feet by 50 feet and 12 knots) followed by the PACIFIC, ARCTIC, and BALTIC (1850) were substantially larger than even the newest Cunarders (AMERICA class, 1,826 tons), surpassing them by over 1,000 tons! Collins also was the proud possessor of a U.S. Post Office mail subsidy of $385,000. When the ATLANTIC made her maiden departure from New York, on April 27, 1850, the American newspapers were generous in their praise, but they had good reason to be. The new liner boasted luxurious private cabins with paneling and damask drapes, a generous-sized dining saloon, steam heat throughout— representing a radical improvement in comfort—and a means by which each occupant of a major cabin could communicate with the steward in order to

The ATLANTIC was the first Collins steamer. At 2,845 tons, 284 feet by 50 feet, and 12 knots, she was substantially larger and faster than the Cunard competition. The Collins steamers proved to be record breakers, but also prone to accident, since they were driven hard. The disastrous losses of the ARCTIC in 1854 and the PACIFIC in 1856, when combined with a reduction in the American subsidy, brought the end of the line in 1858.

obtain service. The result of such luxury was that the Collins Line soon was garnering for itself the cream of the traffic. Jenny Lind, the Swedish Nightingale, crossed on the ATLANTIC during the summer of 1850 and every cabin was booked for that crossing. In Liverpool one of the local newspapers printed a little ditty to the effect that Cunard should charter the Collins ships to pull the Cunarders over. Unfortunately for E. K. Collins, his ships cost substantially more to build than had been expected and much more to maintain in service than had been projected. Furthermore, a series of incidents occurred involving broken paddle blades and broken main shafts. The United States Congress took notice of these factors when it agreed to increase the Collins Line subsidy from $385,000 to $858,000 in return for a biweekly service all year around. An additional stipulation was that the U.S. government could cancel the subsidy at any time on six months notice. On May 10, 1851, the luxurious PACIFIC sailed from New York and thrashed her way across the North Atlantic in the record-breaking time of 9 days, 20 hours, 14 minutes, with 240 passengers—a record-breaking number. Collins ships were carrying an average of 50% more passengers than Cunard. Yet Samuel Cunard was a crafty old fox and had the perspicacity to protect his company's revenues by reaching a working agreement with the Americans. The result was that from May 25, 1850, through March 31, 1855, the vast majority of the income of the two lines was shared on the basis of one-third to Collins and two-thirds to Cunard, an arrangement that supplied Collins with a guaranteed income and share of the trade. The two great rivals were certainly among the most friendly of competitors for the better part of five years until Collins became overwhelmed by adversity.*

It is a fact that the Collins Line ships were driven terribly hard and gangs of workers reportedly swarmed over them whenever they were in New York. Disaster struck on September 27, 1854, when the ARCTIC, nearing Cape Race in dense fog, suddenly collided with the French steamer VESTA. Extending superhuman effort to reach land, the ARCTIC went down nearly five hours later, taking with her somewhere between 285 and 351 individuals out of the 383 on board. Included among those who lost their lives were E. K. Collins' wife, son, and daughter, combining a business catastrophe with a shattering personal loss.

Cunard was not in a position to take the maximum advantage from this situation, since many of their ships had been chartered by the British government as troop transports during the Crimean War (1853–1856)—the first time such assistance was rendered by Cunard. Collins, therefore, was able to continue his business in spite of the disaster. The final blow came when the PACIFIC sailed from Liverpool on January 23, 1856, and was never heard of again. The presumption has always been that the vessel hit an iceberg and

The paddle steamer PERSIA of 1856 was part of the Cunard response to the Collins Line. She was the first iron-hulled mail steamer in the Cunard fleet and marks the critical transition from wood to iron as a building material. This technological advance would make British shipbuilding yards dominant in the world for the next forty years.

*Francis E. Hyde, *Cunard and the North Atlantic, 1840–1973*, MacMillan: London, 1975, pp. 39–45.

went under without a survivor or trace. To his credit E. K. Collins chartered a ship, loaded her with supplies, and sent her out to crisscross the North Atlantic, searching steamer lanes without success. Congress gave notice of reducing the subsidy in August 1857, and the ill-fated Collins Line terminated operations in 1858.

The Cunard Line had elected to meet the threat of the Collins Line ships by building the iron paddle steamer PERSIA (1856). The new liner of 3,300 tons, 376 feet by 45 feet, and $13\frac{1}{2}$ knots was built from the keel up to be a record breaker. She was three times the size of the BRITANNIA, with engines five times as large that burned twice as much coal. She also could carry more than twice as many passengers in luxury equaling that of the Collins Line vessels. The PERSIA soon captured the transatlantic record with a crossing of 9 days, 10 hours, 22 minutes from New York to Liverpool at 13.47 knots, nearly half a knot faster than the best speed of the Collins' paddlers, and regularly improved upon her records. She was the first iron-hulled Cunard mail steamer and marks another major advance in marine technology for the line, although other lines, such as Royal Mail, had pioneered the use of iron.* Wood had become inceasingly unacceptable for oceangoing steam vessels, and for the next 40 years British yards were far ahead of all others in iron and steel shipbuilding. In fact, not until the four-funnel KAISER WILHELM DER GROSSE (1897) was constructed in a German yard for the North German Lloyd was there a non-British-built record breaker.†

The Cunard Line broadened out into other fields of commercial activity besides the North Atlantic. In 1853 ships started to run from Liverpool to the Mediterranean, calling at Gibraltar, Malta, and Istanbul. Initially the arrangement was somewhat informal, but as trade developed the British & Foreign Steam Navigation Company was created, with ownership shared by Samuel Cunard, George Burns, and Charles MacIver, who was rapidly becoming the dominant force on the Liverpool maritime scene. In time the Mediterranean trade represented a substantial percentage of the total income Cunard vessels earned, particularly as the immigrant trade from Southern Europe increased after the American Civil War (1861–1865). Between 1858 and 1861 eight sister ships of around 1,800 tons were constructed for the Mediterranean trade (PALESTINE, OLYMPUS, MARATHON, ATLAS, HECLA, KEDAR, SIDON, and MOROCCO), while five more vessels of 2,000 tons followed in their wake between 1861 and 1863 (TARIFA, TRIPOLI, ALEPPO, MALTA, and PALMYRA). Periodically all these ships, except the MOROCCO, took North Atlantic sailings when trading conditions or need warranted. They all carried a relatively small number of "cabin class" passengers (40–70), but had generous steerage accommodations for 500 or more. The SIDON carried in excess of 300

*N. R. P. Bonsor, *South Atlantic Seaway*, Brookside Publications: Jersey, Channel Islands, 1983, p. 5.
†John H. Shaum, Jr., and William H. Flayhart III, *Majesty at Sea, The Four Stackers*, W. W. Norton, New York, 1981, p. 9.

George Burns (1795–1890) was a Scotsman with shipping interests on both the Clyde and Mersey. When Samuel Cunard needed additional capital to finance the first ships, Robert Napier introduced him to George Burns, who was able to persuade a substantial number of investors to follow his lead.

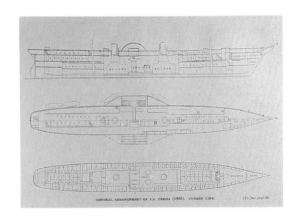

The PERSIA captured the transatlantic record with a crossing of 9 days, 10 hours, 22 minutes from New York to Liverpool at an average speed of 13.47 knots. Last of the Cunard paddle steamers built for the North Atlantic, she was a substantial improvement at 3,300 tons, 376 feet by 45 feet, and 13½ knots.

19

steerage class passengers to New York from Liverpool and Queenstown (Cóbh) in May 1863, and subsequently much greater numbers were common.

Cunard commissioned two outstanding ships in 1862. One, the 3,871-ton paddle steamer SCOTIA, represented the end of an era, since she was the last major ship in the fleet to employ paddles for propulsion, and the other, the 2,638-ton CHINA, was the first Cunard-built mail steamer to be driven by propellers. Cunard had been a little slow in recognizing the superiority of propellers over paddles for first-class tonnage, but by the mid-1860s there remained little doubt about the matter. The huge machinery of the paddlers occupied the prime commercial area of the ship amidships and they required enormous quantities of coal. A propeller-driven vessel was much more economical to run and permitted the positioning of the very best and most expensive cabins in the center section of the ship, an advantage put to use with the advent of the White Star Line in 1870. Furthermore, there was little room left for steerage in a paddle-driven mail steamer, and the immigrant trade could not be ignored. The CHINA, at 326 feet by 40 feet and 2,638 tons, consumed 80 tons of coal a day at 12 knots, whereas the SCOTIA, at 389 feet by 48 feet, burned 387 tons to produce 14 knots. As a return on investment the CHINA could carry 268 cabin and 771 steerage, as well as an additional 1,400 tons of cargo, while the SCOTIA had accommodations for 573 cabin, no steerage passengers, and only 1,050 tons of cargo. The great thrashing paddles of the SCOTIA may have inspired confidence and been impressive, but the slim, screw-propelled hull of the CHINA spelled profits in the Cunard ledgers.

The financial success of the CHINA inspired the Cunard Line to order additional vessels, including the RUSSIA (1867), which was the first screw Cunarder to equal the size and speed of the first-class paddlers (2,960 tons, 358 feet by 43 feet). The new RUSSIA joined the paddlers SCOTIA and the PERSIA in the biweekly service between Liverpool and New York. This combination provided travelers with an interesting opportunity to evaluate paddles versus propellers in relatively equal vessels as part of the premier service of a great North Atlantic line.

The official Cunard mail connection with Boston came to an end in 1867, when the new mail contract, now drawn up by the postmaster general instead of the Admiralty, assigned to Cunard the responsibility of a weekly service from Liverpool via Queenstown to New York in return for a subsidy of £80,000. The Inman Line, a Cunard rival, secured the mail contract for the Liverpool–Boston route, but Cunard did not abandon the port that had treated the line so generously. A biweekly service was initiated with secondary steamers in 1867, and was revised upward to a weekly service in the following year.

Sir Samuel Cunard had been honored by Queen Victoria with a baronetcy in 1858 for his contributions to trade and commerce and for the service of his line to the military in the Crimean War (1853–1856) and the Sepoy (Indian)

Charles MacIver (1811–1885) was a very astute and unrelenting Liverpool shipowner who became a major force in the Cunard Line. In 1878 MacIver was the senior godfather at the birth of the Cunard Steam-Ship Company Limited when the existing partners turned the firm public in order to raise money for new tonnage.

Mutiny (1857), when many ships were used as troop transports and supply vessels. The twenty-fifth anniversary year of the Cunard Line in 1865 brought cause for celebration and cause for sadness. In the same newspaper edition carrying the news of the assassination of President Abraham Lincoln was the obituary of Samuel Cunard, who died on April 28, 1865, at the age of 78. David MacIver, another founder, died in 1845, to be succeeded by his energetic brother Charles. George Burns retired in 1860, although he lived to the advanced age of 95, while Robert Napier reached 86. The two decades between the 1850s and the 1870s saw the creation of a number of formidable rivals to the Cunard Line. In Britain were founded the Inman Line (1850), Anchor Line (1856), Guion Line (1863), and White Star Line (1871). On the continent the Hamburg–American Line started a steamship service in 1856, followed by North German Lloyd (1858), Compagnie Générale Transatlantique (French Line, 1864), Red Star Line, and Holland–America (1873), in the United States the American Line (1873), and in Italy the Navigazione Generale Italiana (1881). None of these companies affected the future of the Cunard Line as much as the founding of the White Star Line. Cunard had lost the Blue Riband to the Inman Line in 1869 after holding it for thirteen years; however, the White Star Line inaugurated a service between Liverpool and New York in 1871 with a fleet of ships having compound engines and passenger accommodations so far ahead of existing standards that they outdated the entire Cunard fleet overnight. Cunard did all they reasonably could in the way of modernizing their existing ships. The HECLA, OLYMPUS, MARATHON, and ATLAS were lengthened by 60 feet, thereby increasing their tonnage to 2,400, and the other ships were fitted with compound engines. Much more important was the commissioning of the 4,550-ton BOTHNIA in 1874 and SCYTHIA in 1875. They were larger but slower than the White Star OCEANIC (1871).*

In due course the Cunard owners met and decided that, in the face of the White Star competition, there was no alternative but to establish a public company. Therefore in 1878 the assets of the founders, or their heirs, in the British and North American Royal Mail Steam Packet Company and in the British & Foreign Steam Navigation Company were transferred to the new Cunard Steam-Ship Company Limited. The partners received stock worth a total of £1,200,000 out of the £2,000,000, and two years later a general offering was made to the British public of the remaining £800,000, which were subscribed immediately. The Cunard prospectus simply stated: "The growing wants of the Company's transatlantic trade demand the acquisition of additional steam ships of great size and power, involving a cost for construction which may best be met by a large public company."[†]

The new influx of capital made it possible in 1881 to order the first steel Cunarder, the 7,392-ton SERVIA (515 feet by 52 feet, 16 knots). The SERVIA

*Bonsor, North Atlantic Seaway, Vol. I, p. 92.
†Cunard Line, The Cunarders 1840–1969, p. 38.

Cunard's safety record over its entire history is little short of phenomenal, since not a single passenger's life has been lost through the company's fault at sea during peacetime. Upon occasions they have been very lucky. The MALTA (1866, 2,132 tons) of the Mediterranean service was lost in a spectacular wreck near Lands End on October 10, 1889, without loss of life.

21

attracted considerable attention when she entered service on 26 November, and received many favorable comments about the luxury of her first-class accommodations. She could carry 480 in first class and as many as 750 in steerage, which was critical to any steamship line's success. The SERVIA was an outstanding Cunard ship, but she actually only followed existing trends. Other liners before her had been built of steel (BUENOS AYREAN, and PARISIAN of the Allan Line) or were larger (CITY OF ROME, 8,415 tons, of the Inman Line) or were faster (ARIZONA, Guion Line). In the luxury of her accommodation the SERVIA approached the ships of the White Star Line, Cunard's closest competitor, and began to lure back some of the customers Cunard had lost in previous years.

The completion of the AURANIA (1883) reinforced the first-class fleet, but this ship certainly experienced some teething troubles. En route to New York on her maiden voyage the AURANIA's engines blew up in mid-Atlantic. Once again, with phenomenal good luck, there was no loss of life. She completed her crossing under sail, ultimately making her maiden arrival in New York Harbor eleven days out from Liverpool with the assistance of three tugs. The damage to her engines was so severe that she was dispatched to Glasgow using only a low-pressure cylinder and did not return to service for nearly a year. After repairs were made, however, she proved herself a worthy addition to the fleet and provided dependable sailings for the next fifteen years.

Cunard occasionally acquired a vessel through luck; this was the case in 1884 when the Guion Line was in severe financial difficulties as a result of the trade depression and could not make the payments to the builders for the new OREGON. Cunard bought the vessel, and she took her maiden sailing for the line on June 8, 1884. The 7,375-ton OREGON was constructed of iron and proved herself a record breaker as she raced outward bound to New York in 6 days, 9 hours, 42 minutes (18.16 knots) on her third Cunard crossing, and home to Liverpool in 6 days, 11 hours, 9 minutes (18.39 knots). The result for Cunard was a record-breaking passenger liner for the first time in fifteen years.

The OREGON (7,374 tons, 501 feet by 54.2 feet, 18 knots) was acquired by the Cunard Line in May 1884 when her owners, the Guion Line, experienced financial difficulties. The OREGON obtained the Blue Riband of the Atlantic for Cunard in August 1884. On March 14, 1886, the liner was in a collision with an unknown sailing vessel 18 miles east of Long Island, N.Y., and sank. All passengers and crew were rescued by the North German Lloyd liner FULDA.

War scares in the mid-1880s occurred all around the British Empire—from the Balkans, to the Middle East, Africa, Northern India, and the Far East. Although no major conflict occurred until World War I, the fact that war clouds often looked so ominous was reason for the Admiralty to charter Cunard vessels, even if on a temporary basis. The OREGON was required for Admiralty service in 1885 as an armed merchant cruiser. When she returned to Cunard, the decision was made that she would open a new express service to Boston once again. The OREGON sailed from Liverpool with nearly 900 passengers on her last scheduled voyage to New York. Approaching Long Island on March 14, 1886, she collided with an unknown sailing ship. The two vessels parted in the fog and the OREGON rapidly began to sink. Fortunately the North German Lloyd steamer FULDA was nearby and she rescued all the passengers and crew of the OREGON, thus preserving the distinguished reputation of the Cunard Line through phenomenal good fortune.

The loss of the OREGON was deeply regretted, but Cunard still had adequate tonnage available. The delivery of the 7,718-ton UMBRIA and ETRURIA in November 1884 and April 1885, respectively, gave them a well-balanced first-class fleet again. Both ships were record breakers and they were the last large greyhounds to have compound engines and only a single propeller. An interesting feature of both ships was that their performances improved with the passage of time. The premier Cunard service from Liverpool to New York was maintained by the excellent quartet of the SERVIA, AURANIA, UMBRIA, and ETRURIA after 1885. This would have been adequate for the next ten years under normal conditions of ship renewal; however, this was not to be the case. Competition on the North Atlantic went wild with the building of new ocean greyhounds, and patrons of the various steamship lines plying these sea-lanes sometimes referred to it as the "frantic Atlantic."

In the mid-1880s the severe economic depression that drove the Guion Line into bankruptcy also threatened the financial stability of the Inman Line, whose founder, William Inman, had died in 1881. Shortly thereafter the Inman Line had taken delivery of the new CITY OF ROME, arguably one of the most beautiful ships ever to cross the Atlantic. Unfortunately the CITY OF ROME, which had been contracted for as a steel-hulled vessel, had been built of iron because of a shortage of the other metal. As a result, she was slower and had a reduced carrying capacity compared with the contract specifications. The Inman Line, in the uncertainty following William Inman's death, returned the ship to the builders and refused to accept her. The fortunes of the line deteriorated substantially in the economic depression of the next four years, and their ships fell far behind those of Cunard and White Star, the other Liverpool shipping giants. Some discussion took place between T. H. Ismay of White Star and other Liverpool shipowners about saving the Inman Line. Ismay reportedly was ready to loan as much as £1,000,000 to the bankrupt

The publications of steamship lines provide a valuable description of their services. In 1897 Cunard was operating a fleet of twenty-four vessels in addition to other tonnage chartered when needed.

company, but Cunard and others were unwilling.* The idea behind Ismay's charity was "never to let a weak man out of your trade, thus letting a strong one in." This doctrine was verified when Clement Acton Griscom, the Philadelphia shipping magnate, succeeded in gaining control of the Inman Line and the company was reborn as the Inman & International Steamship Company Ltd. (1886). The rejuvenated steamship line went to its builders for two greatly improved vessels, the CITY OF NEW YORK (1888), and the CITY OF PARIS (1889), which in turn forced Cunard and White Star to build when neither really wanted to have the expense. In the long run it probably would have been far less of a financial strain to have kept the Inman Line in operation.

Cunard immediately retaliated against the new American owners of the Inman Line by insisting that they would have nothing to do with any postal contract that involved that line. Critical discussions followed during which Cunard was warned it might be sued for failing to carry the mails, but the line held firm and was supported by White Star. The subsequent mail contract called for a reduction of the official sailings from Liverpool from three a week to twice weekly, with the Tuesday Inman sailing eliminated, the White Star Thursday sailing switched to Wednesday, and the Cunard Saturday departure remaining fixed. The refusal to share the postal revenues in some ways backfired on the British Lines, because it led to the creation of the rejuvenated American Line of 1893, and ultimately to J. P. Morgan's huge American shipping trust, the International Mercantile Marine, in 1902.

The new ships ordered by the American Line forced Cunard as well as the other major shipping lines back to their builders for new tonnage. The result for Cunard was the commissioning of the 12,950-ton twin-screw CAMPANIA and LUCANIA in 1893. These famous ships were propelled by twin sets of five-cylinder, triple-expansion engines that were so large that their engine rooms were virtual cathedrals of the Industrial Revolution. They were the first Cunarders to dispense with sails as a safety measure. The CAMPANIA and LUCANIA were designed to take all the luxury of a wealthy Victorian home to sea: solid paneling, heavy brocade, rich wood carvings, stained glass windows, and palm trees. These two impressive ships were very popular with the elite traveling public. Cunard Line brochures of the 1890s stressed the fact that the CAMPANIA and LUCANIA could provide the ultimate luxury of "privacy" for the single person in that they were fitted with a number of single-berth cabins. In earlier ships, even in first class, a single passenger frequently had to share a cabin with another traveler and be faced with the "luck of the draw." Most travelers still expected to share facilities, but at least the option (at an appropriate surcharge) of complete privacy was available. Another first for Cunard was the provision of suites consisting of a single or double cabin with

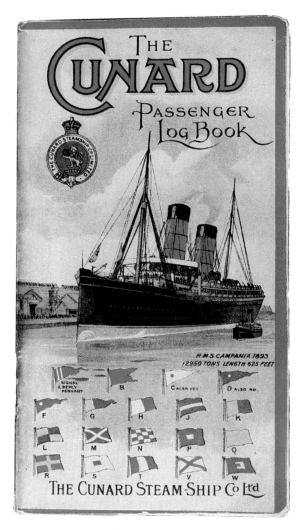

The Cunard Passenger Log Book for 1897 is graced with a drawing of the CAMPANIA (1893, 12,950 tons), which, with her sister ship LUCANIA (1893, 12,952 tons) and the UMBRIA (1884, 7,718 tons) and ETRURIA (1885, 7,718 tons), maintained the first-class North Atlantic service. These ships all were capable of regular crossings at 19–21 knots, and the CAMPANIA and LUCANIA were among the fastest Atlantic liners from 1893 to 1897.

24

*Roy Anderson, WHITE STAR, T. Stephenson & Sons Ltd.: Prescot, Lancashire, 1964, p. 87.

an adjoining sitting room. The popularity of the "Suites" among the wealthiest clientele made them a planned part of future tonnage.

The CAMPANIA and LUCANIA proved themselves fast and solid performers. The CAMPANIA was responsible for the fastest maiden voyage on record in April 1893, and for regaining the eastbound Blue Riband for the Cunard Line by sailing home in 5 days, 17 hours, 27 minutes at an average speed of 21.30 knots, followed by a record 21.12 knots westbound. The two ships were very well balanced and frequently averaged over 21 knots both westbound and eastbound over many successive voyages. Of the two ships, the LUCANIA was slightly faster. Such dependability earned the respect of the public and brought dividends, although the competition between Cunard and White Star in Liverpool and the American Line ships sailing from Southampton frequently was cutthroat. Furthermore, the challenge of the continental lines such as HAPAG, North German Lloyd, and the Compagnie Générale Transatlantique was becoming increasingly acute. Cunard was impressed by the competition, but the firm's first priority was to make a profit, not record breakers. The latter were exceedingly costly to build, maintain, and operate, rarely making money unless they were integrated into a carefully developed fleet program.

The premier new ships of the Cunard fleet at the turn of the century were the 14,000-ton IVERNIA and SAXONIA specifically designed for the Liverpool–Boston trade, where they proved themselves to be among the most popular ships of any fleet on the North Atlantic. At 15 knots no speed record was threatened, but the IVERNIA and SAXONIA, sporting the tallest single funnels ever given a North Atlantic steamer (106 feet), had accommodations in three classes for 1,964 passengers. On April 23, 1901, when a large number of small children and infants were being carried, the SAXONIA sailed from Liverpool with the astonishing number of 2,260 souls on the passenger list! She and the IVERNIA were among the most profitable single ships in the Cunard fleet.

The creation of John Pierpont Morgan's International Mercantile Marine Corporation in the period 1901–1903 placed a premium on the Cunard Line as the White Star Line and numerous other British concerns either were bought by the IMM or signed agreements with the shipping trust. Even Albert Ballin of the gigantic German HAPAG agreed to reduce competition with J. P. Morgan. Cunard felt the pressure acutely and approached the British government with the proposition that the line would build two new contestants for the Atlantic record and remain both a British-flag and British-owned company if the government would extend assistance in financing the needed tonnage. The alternative was the selling out of the last major British steamship line on the North Atlantic, to foreigners. After a considerable period of hard negotiating the British government agreed to assist the Cunard Line with the necessary financing of the proposed superships, provided that they remained British in every way and would be available to the Admiralty whenever needed.

Having arranged financing, Cunard's next major problem was the character of the propulsion system for new ships. Should they involve the traditional reciprocating engines or the still novel Parsons turbines? The decision was made to experiment in two similar ships with the different propulsion systems. Two large intermediate steamers were ordered for delivery in 1905, the CARMANIA and the CARONIA (20,000 tons, 650 feet by 72 feet, 18 knots). The CARMANIA was constructed with the new steam turbines and proved herself to be appreciably faster and somewhat less expensive to run, depending on the demands placed upon her. As a result, Cunard became daring in the conception of its fleet for the first time since Samuel Cunard ordered the initial quartet and decided to build two giant liners powered with the largest turbines then available. Technology was stretched to the limits in the creation of these ships. The contract for one of the liners was won by John Brown on the Clyde, and the other went to Swan, Hunter & Wigham Richardson on the Tyne.

June 7, 1906, marked a milestone not only in the history of the Cunard Line, but also in the entire development of the transatlantic ferry. On that day John Brown launched the LUSITANIA, and instantly all the first-class tonnage on the North Atlantic became obsolete. The LUSITANIA was the largest ship in the world at 31,550 tons with a length of 762 feet and a breadth of 88 feet. She had accommodations for 563 in first, 464 in second, and 1,138 in third class, and sailed at capacity on her maiden voyage September 7, 1907. Superlatives greeted her wherever she went, and she fulfilled the expectations of her owners and builders by making the fastest crossing of the Atlantic in both directions during October 1807 at speeds of 23.99 knots westbound and 23.61 knots eastbound. The "LUCY" thus became the first ship to take the Atlantic crossing under five days, even if only by fractions and from Queenstown. The MAURETANIA followed after some adjustments for vibration and soon proved herself a worthy consort to her sister. The two ships exchanged the Blue Riband back and forth for nearly two years until the installation of new propellers to the MAURETANIA gave her an advantage over the LUCY. With a record passage of 4 days, 10 hours, 51 minutes at an average speed of 26.06 knots over a distance of 2,784 miles from Queenstown to New York, the MAURETANIA created a record that would stand for 20 years. If the LUSITANIA was "the" ship as the first of the new class of superliners, the "MAURY" became one of the most popular and beloved ships ever to grace the North Atlantic, and enjoyed a very full career, from 1907 to 1935.

The loss of the aging LUCANIA through a fire while in the Huskisson Dock, Liverpool, in August 1909 underlined the need for a third vessel to partner the big two. Accordingly, Cunard ordered a slightly larger but slower version of their two speed queens, thus creating the "Ship Beautiful" AQUITANIA. She was one of the largest ships in the world, at 45,647 tons, when delivered in 1914. Basically, she was a LUSITANIA with an extra deck, but had a standard of appointments that made her one of the most distinguished ships of her era.

The CARMANIA (1905, 19,524 tons) was a large intermediate liner built for the Cunard Line and outfitted with the "new" steam turbines as a working experiment. Her sister ship, CARONIA (1905, 19,687 tons), was given quadruple expansion engines. The end result was that the CARMANIA was ¾ knot faster, or slightly cheaper to operate at the same speed. Accordingly, the decision was made to equip the two new giant Cunarders with turbines.

The CARPATHIA (1903, 13,555 tons) carried cargo, 204 second-class, and 1,500 third-class passengers. After Cunard became the official agent of the Hungarian government for immigration in 1903, she was employed extensively in the immigrant trade between Trieste on the Adriatic and New York. On the night of April 12, 1912, CARPATHIA was outward bound from New York to the Mediterranean when she heard the distress signal of the giant White Star liner TITANIC and went to her aid. All of the 700 survivors were rescued by her.

The IVERNIA and SAXONIA (1900, 14,058 and 14,281 tons, respectively) were two large intermediate liners created for the Liverpool–Boston service. Liverpool was the Cunard European terminus, but the tide conditions in the Mersey made it difficult for larger ships to come alongside the pier on many occasions.

Her speed of 23 knots made it possible to deliver her passengers (597 in first, 614 in second, and 2,052 in third—over 1,000 more than her swifter consorts) to New York in a balanced three-ship schedule with the LUSITANIA and MAURETANIA. The basic idea was to have one ship ready to sail from Liverpool, one ready to sail from New York, and one in mid-Atlantic, thereby maintaining the weekly sailing schedule from both sides of the Atlantic.

The AQUITANIA barely had time to complete three voyages in 1914 before the beginning of World War I plunged Britain into the first general European war in ninety-nine years. She was requisitioned for duty as an armed merchant cruiser, but this service was short-lived because her size made her too vulnerable. Furthermore, on August 25, 1914, the AQUITANIA returned to Liverpool with heavy damage to her bow as the result of a collision with the Leyland liner CANADIAN off the Old Head of Kinsale, Ireland. The LUSITANIA had sailed from New York in pitch darkness at 0100 hours on August 5 and made a fast crossing to England. There were thousands of Americans caught in Europe as a result of the declaration of war, and the decision was made to use the LUSITANIA and the MAURETANIA to carry tourists and others back to the United States during the fall of 1914. Then the MAURETANIA joined the AQUITANIA in lay-up until a satisfactory employment for these valuable ships could be found.

The LUSITANIA maintained a reduced Cunard sailing schedule by herself for the first few months of 1915. Her last sailing from New York started on May 1, 1915, with 1,959 passengers and crew onboard. Five days later, as the big Cunarder approached the Irish Coast near the Old Head of Kinsale, she was torpedoed by the German submarine U-20 and went down with 1,198 of those who had sailed with her. The subsequent international furor over unrestricted submarine warfare contributed to the American decision to enter World War I on the side of the Allies in April 1917 after Germany resumed such activity.

The LUSITANIA (1907, 31,550 tons) remains one of the most famous of all Cunarders. She was the first of the giant trio built by the line between 1907 and 1914 to maintain the first-class service. A highly successful vessel, she captured the Blue Riband in October 1907 with an average speed of 23.99 knots. After eight years of commercial service she was torpedoed on May 7, 1915, off the Irish coast and went down with 1,198 in twenty minutes.

In May 1915 the MAURETANIA and the AQUITANIA were converted into troopships for use in the Mediterranean in support of the ill-fated Dardanelles campaign. Following their trooping duties both ships also served for a period as hospital ships, painted white with great red crosses emblazoned on their sides and sporting buff funnels. Subsequently both ships served as troopships for the Canadian forces bound to Europe and then, after April 1917, for the American Expeditionary Force as it crossed to France. Immediately following the armistice the steamship lines were desperate for tonnage, and as quickly as possible the MAURETANIA and AQUITANIA were returned to Cunard to handle the flood of travelers trying to cross the Atlantic. It was decided that they would partially replace the prewar German lines in the South-ampton–Cherbourg–New York trade, the first such sailing being taken by the AQUITANIA on June 14, 1919. Both ships required extensive renovation of all passenger accommodations and a total overhaul of their machinery after the rigors of wartime service. The decision was made to convert both ships from coal to oil, which eliminated the horrendous labor of coaling the giant liners in port and of maintaining the coal-fired boilers at sea. In fact, the crews of the ships were reduced from 350 to 50 in the "stokers" category.

The loss of the LUSITANIA might have made Cunard short of first-class tonnage for the three-ship service if it had not been possible to acquire the ex-HAPAG liner IMPERATOR (1913, 52,226 tons, 883 feet by 98 feet), which was renamed the BERENGARIA. The IMPERATOR and her sister ship BISMARCK were both assigned as war reparations to Britain after World War I and were jointly bought by Cunard and White Star in order to avoid outbidding each other. This cooperative effort remained in force for approximately ten years, although each line assumed complete control of its own vessel. White Star renamed their ship the MAJESTIC, but she only had one suitable running mate, the OLYMPIC. Cunard, therefore, had the best-balanced trio of giant ships on the Atlantic from 1919 to 1935 with the MAURETANIA, AQUITANIA, and BERENGARIA.

The 1920s saw Cunard rebuilding its fleet, but with great caution, since the revision of the American immigration laws all but eliminated the need for steerage. In the place of the immigrant trade, which was drastically reduced, came an ever-increasing group of American tourists. Parts of the third-class quarters were modified and upgraded as tourist third cabin (later called tourist class) in recognition of this increase. The 1920s were not a boom time everywhere, and competition on the North Atlantic for travelers was fierce. As a result, much wider use of vessels for cruising came into vogue, particularly during the winter months. By the late 1920s the introduction of new first-class tonnage by German and Italian lines emphasized the need for Cunard to complete plans for the next generation of superliners. When White Star ordered a 60,000-ton ship and the French Line signed a contract for an 80,000-ton vessel, time became critical. Insofar as Cunard was concerned, the ultimate North Atlantic service appeared obtainable.

The BERENGARIA (1920, 52,226 tons, 22 knots) was launched as the HAPAG IMPERATOR in 1912, but was never completed because of World War I. After the war she became the Cunard BEREGARIA, named for the wife of Richard I, the "lion hearted." As such she was the largest Cunarder and replaced the lost LUSITANIA in the weekly express service.

In 1840 Samuel Cunard had built a fleet of four ships in order to ensure regular service across the Atlantic. Initially biweekly, the service soon was established on a weekly basis, with ships sailing from either side of the Atlantic on a given day each week. Throughout the intervening ninety years every major advance in marine technology had resulted in larger, faster, and *fewer* ships to maintain the first-class service. By 1893 the UMBRIA, ETRURIA, CAMPANIA, and LUCANIA were capable of maintaining Cunard's weekly sailings. By 1907 it was possible for Cunard to think in terms of three ships for the first-class service from Britain to the United States, and the LUSITANIA, MAURETANIA, and later the AQUITANIA had been born. Now in the late 1920s the ultimate service appeared to be within the grasp of Cunard. The possibility existed because of advances in marine technology of building two giant superliners that would be both large enough and fast enough to maintain the weekly sailings by themselves: two great liners sailing from Europe and America each week, passing each other in a majestic and thrilling mid-Atlantic meeting (weather and course permitting), and racing on to their destinations at nearly 30 knots. The vision was heroic; the realization in the face of the Great Depression would be extremely difficult.

The keel of an 80,000-ton Cunard liner was laid at John Brown's Shipyard on the Clyde, December 12, 1930, and given the yard number 534. Work proceeded on the enormous hull until December 10, 1931, when construction was suspended as a direct result of the economic devastation of the depression. Cunard could not build the ship without passenger and freight revenue, and trade on the North Atlantic had virtually dried up. The colossal hull of 534 rusting away on the Scottish slip was a gaunt reminder of how bad economic conditions were. Under the pressure of the depression, steamship lines collapsed in many trades. White Star had become British owned again after World War I, but was undercapitalized and began to go bankrupt as the depression deepened. When Cunard approached the British government for aid in completing No. 534 and an appropriate sister ship, the terms offered involved a merger of the two foremost British-flag North Atlantic lines. In February 1934 the Cunard–White Star Line was created, and work resumed on No. 534 in April, with the proposed launching date scheduled for September 26, 1934. Considerable excitement above and beyond the usual surrounded the launching. The merger of Cunard and White Star created a potential problem in naming the new ship, since all Cunard vessels ended in IA and all White Star ships ended in IC. Few guessed the solution that had been devised until Her Majesty Queen Mary ascended to the launching platform and at the appointed time in the rain-soaked ceremony christened the giant hull QUEEN MARY. A gracious monarch had consented to give the new superliner her own name in recognition of the fact that the ship had become a symbol of national unity and determination in the face of the dark clouds of the depression.

The merger of Cunard and White Star required drastic rationalization of the combined fleet. In the depths of the depression it was difficult enough to maintain a single first-class fleet, let alone twice the tonnage. The MAURETANIA was withdrawn from service in the fall of 1934, the OLYMPIC in the spring of 1935, and the MAJESTIC and HOMERIC early in 1936, while the BERENGARIA, AQUITANIA, and QUEEN MARY maintained the service from 1936 to 1938.

The QUEEN MARY's maiden voyage from Southampton to New York began on May 27, 1936, with an intermediate stop at Cherbourg. Wherever she went, the new liner was greeted by crowds and unprecedented enthusiasm. Her entry into New York was a publicity triumph, with the superliner accepting the thunderous salutes of all the vessels in the harbor and a flotilla of escorts seeing her to her North River pier. The QUEEN MARY overwhelmingly was the largest British-flag ship at 80,774 tons and with a length of 1,019 feet, 5 inches and a breadth of 118 feet, 6 inches. These statistics also compared

The MAURETANIA (1907, 31,938 tons) was the second of the Cunard big three before World War I. Entering service two months after the LUSITANIA, she proved herself slightly faster and would hold the Blue Riband from 1907 to 1929. A consistent performer between 1909 and 1911, she averaged well over 25 knots for forty-four round voyages.

The AQUITANIA (1914, 45,647 tons) was the third of the giant Cunarders before World War I. Basically a LUSITANIA with an additional deck, the AQUITANIA was the epitome of luxury, even if slightly slower, at 23 knots, than her consorts. She fitted into the three-ship service beautifully and would survive to serve in both World Wars being scrapped only in 1950.

31

very favorably with her greatest competitor, the giant NORMANDIE of the French Line, which emerged from the builder's yard at 79,280 tons, 1,029 feet, 4 inches by 117 feet by 9 inches but whose tonnage subsequently was increased by various modifications to 83,423. The NORMANDIE had taken her maiden sailing from Le Havre on May 29, 1935, nearly a year ahead of the QUEEN MARY; construction of the liner had not been interrupted thanks to the French government's assistance. The NORMANDIE took the Blue Riband of the North Atlantic in 1935 with crossing of 4 days, 3 hours, 2 minutes westbound (29.98 knots) and 4 days, 3 hours, 25 minutes eastbound (30.31 knots). The French liner thus became the first vessel to push the speed over 30 knots for an entire Atlantic crossing, and the QUEEN MARY faced a real challenge.

When pressed about the record, Cunard found it necessary to state that their new liner would not compete for the Blue Riband, but simply would seek to perform up to the highest standards consistent with a regular service. On the crossings of August 20–24, 1936 (westbound), and August 26–30 (eastbound), the QUEEN MARY steamed across from Bishops Rock to Ambrose in 4 days, 27 minutes (30.14 knots) and returned in 3 days, 23 hours, 57 minutes (30.63 knots), becoming the first ship ever to complete back-to-back 30-knot crossings and the first vessel to lower the time below 4 days for a crossing. Thereafter the QUEEN MARY and the NORMANDIE exchanged the Blue Riband between them before the Cunarder proved herself the faster in 1938 by a fraction of a knot. The French Line announced the building of a slightly larger and faster consort for the NORMANDIE, with construction to begin in 1940, but by then World War II was underway.

Cunard had received sufficient funds to underwrite the building of the sister ship to the QUEEN MARY, and the keel of this vessel was laid on December 4, 1936, at John Brown's. The launching of the new liner occurred after the accession of King George VI and Queen Elizabeth (the Queen Mother), and the new Queen was asked by Cunard to launch the second liner.

The QUEEN MARY (1936; 80,774 tons, 29 knots) was described as the "smallest and slowest" ship capable of maintaining the weekly express service between Southampton and New York with only one consort. The liner was built at John Brown & Co., Ltd., on the Clyde and launched by Her Majesty Queen Mary on September 26, 1934. The merger of the Cunard and White Star lines as a result of the depression had produced some excitement about the name of the new liner. The name QUEEN MARY was highly appropriate.

Accordingly, on September 27, 1938, Queen Elizabeth came to Clydebank and gave her name to the new ship as QUEEN ELIZABETH.

In September 1939 a world war interrupted regular Cunard services for the second time in the century. The QUEEN MARY was immediately taken over as a fast troopship and the QUEEN ELIZABETH was still being fitted out on the Clyde in Scotland. She was too valuable to remain in that vulnerable position, and at the earliest possible opportunity she sailed for "trials" on March 2, 1940, which resulted in her safe arrival at New York five days later. The NORMANDIE of the French Line, the giant rival of the QUEENS, had been requisitioned by the U.S. government and renamed the U.S.S. LAFAYETTE. She caught fire at her pier in New York in January 1942 and never returned to service. Between them, the two QUEENS ferried 320,000 of the 865,000 U.S. troops landed in Britain before the invasion of Europe. General Dwight D. Eisenhower credited the two giant Cunarders with shortening the war in Europe by a full year through their unique ability to transport 15,000 troops at a time. The loan of the two largest ships in the world by Britain to the United States constituted a significant reverse "lend–lease" factor during World War II and a major contribution on the part of Britain to the American war effort. Together the two QUEENS carried the astonishing number of 1,622,054 passengers during the war years and steamed 1,150,406 miles.

While all of the Cunard fleet was involved in the war, two ships rendered major service: the new intermediate liner MAURETANIA, 35,738 tons, which had entered service in 1939 and been given the name of her famous predecessor, and the aging AQUITANIA, which would have been retired when the QUEEN ELIZABETH entered service had the war not intervened. The old AQUITANIA became the only major ship of the Cunard Fleet to serve in both World War I and II, continuing her service until 1950.

As soon as possible after the war, Cunard refurbished the QUEENS, and in 1946 the two-ship transatlantic service became a reality with the QUEEN MARY and the QUEEN ELIZABETH. Sir Percy Bates, the chairman of Cunard–White Star whose vision had seen the creation of the two QUEENS, collapsed and died at Southampton shortly after the maiden sailing of the QUEEN ELIZABETH from her home port on October 16, 1946. When entering the regular North Atlantic service of the Cunard Line in 1946, the QUEEN ELIZABETH, at 83,673 tons, 1,031 feet by 118 feet, 6 inches held the distinction of being the largest passenger liner ever built. The QUEEN MARY and the QUEEN ELIZABETH maintained Cunard's first-class service for the next 21 years and established an enviable record of popularity. The total number of passengers carried by the QUEEN ELIZABETH during her first full year in service was 102,292 passengers during the course of 23 round trips—an average of 2,224 per trip! The healthy financial picture of the Cunard Line in 1949 permitted them to buy out the remaining White Star interest and change the name back to the Cunard Steam-Ship Company Limited. The BRITANNIC (1930), (26,943 tons,

712 feet overall by 83 feet), last of the White Star ships, retained the buff funnels with the black crown of White Star until she was retired in 1960, but little else remained of what once had been one of the world's foremost steamship lines.

The MAURETANIA was reconditioned and rejoined the fleet in April 1947, while new tonnage included the 13,345-ton MEDIA, the first new postwar passenger vessel; a sister ship, the PARTHIA; and the spectacular 34,183-ton CARONIA, in 1949. Other prewar ships that slowly returned to commercial activity were the ASCANIA (14,013 tons), BRITANNIC (revised tonnage 27,650), SAMARIA (19,602 tons), SCYTHIA (19,730 tons), and FRANCONIA (20,158 tons). The French terminal at Cherbourg was repaired after war damage by May of 1952, and continental passengers could now embark directly on to the biggest Cunarders without the use of tenders to ferry them out to the ships. A new train, "The Cunarder," was created to run between Waterloo Station, London, and the Southampton docks in order to expedite the movement of thousands of passengers to the ships. It began service for the July 2, 1952, sailing. The departure of The Cunarder from the cavernous Waterloo Station always was a dramatic moment as the distinguished bass voice of the train announcer indicated that the boat train for R.M.S. QUEEN MARY, sailing from Southampton to New York was about to leave. The excitement was incalculably enhanced if other liners also were sailing and a long series of boat trains for other ships were being called. The train ride through the rolling English countryside to the Southampton docks provided a brief interlude and a means of catching one's breath for the thrill of embarkation on a ship that had come to be so much more than a living bit of history and tradition.

In the early 1950s Cunard also ordered a quartet of 22,000-ton liners, SAXONIA (1954), IVERNIA (1955), CARINTHIA (1956), and SYLVANIA (1957), all of which were intended for use in a service between Britain, Quebec, and Montreal, although they took some New York sailings during the winter months. The interior fittings of the quartet were luxurious for the 110–154 first-class passengers, but out of step for the times in connection with the 800 tourist-class cabins, most of which lacked private facilities. Cunard realized this, and during 1963 the SAXONIA and IVERNIA were refurbished as cruising liners with greatly refined accommodations. They were renamed CARMANIA and FRANCONIA and were painted in the light-green cruising colors made popular by the CARONIA. The CARINTHIA and the SYLVANIA were laid up in 1967 and then sold to the Sitmar Line in 1968 to become the FAIRSEA and the FAIRWIND. The CARMANIA and the FRANCONIA proved to be popular Bermuda and Caribbean cruise liners, but a combination of labor problems and the rising cost of fuel forced their retirement in 1971. Ultimately they were sold to the Soviet Union in 1973 and renamed the LEONID SOBINOV and FEDOR SHALYAPIN. The earning capacity of the Canadian quartet was severely affected by the advent of jet aircraft after 1958, as were the revenues from the QUEENS.

The year 1958 was the last time that more passengers crossed the North Atlantic by sea than by air. The Industrial Revolution as applied to transportation made another great leap forward as 3½-day Blue Riband passages, even by the superliner UNITED STATES, which in 1952 took the record from the QUEEN MARY, became inconsequential in the face of air flights reckoned in hours. At the same time the policies of the British government toward taxation of business profits and the reserves necessary to finance new construction continuously wore down the resources of an old established firm like Cunard. The Cunard Steam-Ship Company began to lose money on its passenger operations at an ever-increasing rate. Drastic actions had to be taken in many areas, but the most critical problem facing the line in the early 1960s was what action to take with the first-class North Atlantic service. The QUEEN MARY and QUEEN ELIZABETH remained remarkable vessels, but they were aging and their fuel consumption at nearly 1,000 tons a day represented an enormous expense.

One set of plans for a new liner had been created in the late 1950s, and the ship had been dubbed Q3. If built, that liner would have been around 75,000 tons and basically a modernized version of the QUEENS. The times had changed radically, however, and the Q3 design was scrapped in favor of a slightly smaller and more versatile vessel capable of alternating at will between the North Atlantic and cruising—the Q4. John Brown and Company won the contract, which was signed on December 30, 1964, and the ship was laid

The QUEEN MARY has inspired many artists, but this painting by John Nicholson of Leeds ranks as one of the best. She is shown at sea on the North Atlantic, steaming along at 29 knots on a normal 4½-day crossing. She would maintain the weekly service in peacetime from 1936 to 1967, when she was retired and sold to the city of Long Beach, California, for use as a maritime museum and hotel.

The QUEEN ELIZABETH (1940, 83,673 tons) was the largest passenger liner ever built. She was designed as a steamlined consort for the QUEEN MARY, the second giant ship for the weekly service. She was due to enter service in 1940, when World War II intervened and her first crossing of the Atlantic was a secret dash from Scotland to New York. Subsequently she and the QUEEN MARY carried as many as 16,000 souls per voyage and were credited by Eisenhower with shortening the war in Europe by a full year.

The CARONIA (34,183 tons, 715 feet by 91 feet, 22 knots) was Cunard's "Green Goddess," built especially as a luxurious long cruise liner and only occasionally serving on the North Atlan-tic. The CARONIA took Cunard's World Cruise, or long cruise, every year from her commissioning in 1949 through 1967 and was the largest unit of postwar fleet prior to the QE2.

down on July 5, 1965—almost exactly 125 years after the maiden sailing of the BRITANNIA. Plans were made to rationalize the fleet to recognize the financial facts of the maritime world. In line with this, the MAURETANIA was scrapped in the fall of 1965. Matters worsened before the new construction could be completed, and Sir Basil Smallpeice, who had strong business experience, was brought in as chairman of Cunard in November 1965. In order to raise additional funds, the Cunard headquarters were transferred from Liverpool to London, and the Cunard buildings in Liverpool, London, and New York were sold, while Cunard ticket offices were replaced by agencies in many cities. The 1965 figures revealed that Cunard had lost £2,700,000 on passenger ship operations and made only £900,000 on freight operations, for a net loss of £1,800,000. No company could stand that strain, finance a new ship, and still survive. Accordingly, the difficult decision was made to withdraw the QUEEN MARY at the end of the 1967 summer season and the QUEEN ELIZABETH late in 1968 just prior to delivery of the new ship.

The QUEEN MARY brought the astonishing sum of £1,230,000 when sold to the city of Long Beach, California. She sailed from Southampton for the last time on September 16, 1967, with 1,040 passengers on board for a cruise to California around Cape Horn (she could not transit the Panama Canal). The Cunard "Green Goddess" CARONIA also was retired in November 1967 and led a checkered life until sold for scrapping in 1974, only to be wrecked and sunk at Guam during a storm while under tow to a Chinese yard. The QUEEN ELIZABETH maintained the North Atlantic service by herself during 1968, alternating sailings with the FRANCE of the French Line in a gentlemen's agreement not to have both big ships on the same side of the Atlantic. She was withdrawn from service on November 4, 1968, and sold to a group who intended to use her as a floating attraction in Port Everglades, Florida. This ultimately collapsed, as did a subsequent venture, and finally the ship was of-fered for auction. It looked as though she would be scrapped when C. Y. Tung, the Hong Kong shipping magnate, bought her. Tung intended to renovate and refurbish her as a floating university and rename her SEAWISE UNIVERSITY. The reconstruction was nearly complete when a mysterious fire broke out on January 9, 1972, and the giant liner turned on her side and burned for days in Hong Kong Harbor, becoming a total loss. She has since been completely scrapped—an unfortunate end for the largest passenger liner ever built.

The drastic fleet rationalization on the part of Cunard was the only option open to the line if it was going to survive. Time, money, and changing tastes were telling arguments against the older units, as well as the enormous rise in fuel costs, which would be even more critical in the decade to come. By late 1968 the fortunes, future, and survival of the Cunard Steam-Ship Company lay with the spectacular new QUEEN ELIZABETH 2.

CHAPTER TWO

A Queen Is Born:
The Ordering and
Building
of the QE2

*The keel laying for Yard No. 736 was
scheduled for July 2, 1965, but the
180-ton block of steel involving three keel
sections welded together would not budge
on that day, and the cranes began to
move instead. Nevertheless, the keel-
laying ceremony went ahead as scheduled
at John Brown's, even though the plate
actually was shifted onto the blocks three
days later. (Photo courtesy of the John
Maxtone-Graham Collection.)*

The decision to invest $70,000,000 in a project certainly never would be an easy one to make. When an industry is under acute stress as the result of changes beyond its control and a revolutionary new approach to design and technology is required, the strain of such a move would be tremendous. This was the situation when the Cunard management faced the issue of what type of vessel should replace the QUEEN MARY and the QUEEN ELIZABETH in the late 1950s and early 1960s.

Official public notice of plans to replace the QUEENS occurred on April 8, 1959, when Harold Watkinson, of the ministry of transport, announced to the House of Commons that negotiations were underway with Cunard to try to maintain the first-class North Atlantic service. The previous month Colonel Denis H. Bates told the Annual Meeting of Cunard that the entire future of the North Atlantic service had been placed before the government. Particular notice was taken of the fact that the U.S. government built the liner UNITED STATES at a cost in excess of $75,000,000 and then made the vessel available to the U.S. Lines, Cunard's competition, for less than $34,000,000. "Faced with the overwhelming odds of ever-increasing governmental subsidies to our competitors on the score of national prestige," Bates commented, "your board have decided it is impossible to continue under such unequal and unfair competition to free enterprise." The QUEENS were described as "full of life," but they could not be run forever, and the QUEEN MARY probably would be well over thirty before her replacement would take to sea. Competitively that was not advantageous to the Cunard Line.

The official government group given the responsibility for evaluating the situation was the Chandos committee, which began with the assumption that two liners ultimately would be built to replace the QUEENS and maintain the existing service. The recommendation of the Chandos committee on June 1, 1960, was in favor of government support for the construction of a 75,000-ton liner with a length of 990 feet and a service speed of $29\frac{1}{2}$ knots capable of carrying 2,270 passengers. The estimated cost in 1959 was £25 million to £30 million, with up to £18 million being provided by a low-interest government loan. On October 10, 1960, some five months later, Ernest Marples, then minister of transport, announced the government's acceptance of the recommendations of the Chandos committee. Vociferous opposition occurred almost immediately from some members of Parliament who regarded the loan as an unprecedented subsidy, and from a vocal group of Cunard stockholders who regarded the building of another giant Atlantic liner in the face of competition from the jet airplane as insane. The critics contended that to build another traditional liner in the face of the changing nature of the transportation and travel industries was to fly in the face of common sense and reality. Certainly the Q3, as the new liner was dubbed, would enjoy only limited cruising flexibility during the winter months. The winter payloads on the older QUEENS already were reduced virtually to nothing, and every time such a unit left port, she was destined to cast off into a sea of red ink. On one occasion the giant QUEEN ELIZABETH made a winter crossing with only sixty-three passengers.

The whole complexion of the North Atlantic was undergoing radical change. In 1957 the division of passengers between ships and airlines was roughly 50%–50%. By 1965 the ratio had changed to an astonishing 14%–86% and the number of individuals crossing by sea had dropped from over 1 million to around 650,000. In the same period the airlines saw their figures soar to over 4 million as the jets reduced the Atlantic crossing to a matter of hours. Even the British government investment concessions after 1957 which allowed a company to take investment tax credits meant little, because the Cunard Line had to earn substantial profits in order to make additional investments and thus take advantage of the new arrangement. Those days of high profits were gone forever with the existing fleet.

Cunard endeavored to place itself in a more favorable position by acquiring British Eagle Airways in 1959, but that concern ran afoul of the government policy to restrict competition with BOAC in 1961. Subsequently Cunard and BOAC reached a trading agreement that created BOAC–CUNARD to operate the principal British-flag air service on the North Atlantic. Cunard owned 30% of the new concern and enjoyed an increasing profit in the period between 1962–1965. By 1965 it was clear that a substantial new investment was going to be necessary to maintain a competitive edge in air travel. Cunard could not build a new liner and order new airplanes at the same time. An agreement was reached in 1966 for BOAC to purchase Cunard's share of their joint operations at a price of £11½ million in cash that freed Cunard's assets and saved the company from an additional cash drain. Unfortunately between 1960 and 1965 the passenger ships of the line had lost £14.1 million, which was only partially offset by tax refunds. A total rethinking of the future of the maritime industry and Cunard's role in it was imperative. The debate over the nature of the new vessel must be considered against this background of financial crisis.

The introduction of the magnificent FRANCE of the French Line in 1962 and the pairing of that vessel with the UNITED STATES of the U.S. Lines provided additional competition for the QUEENS. Cunard countered by having the QUEENS skip their annual summer refit, which prior to this had cost them a round trip in the height of the season. This added appreciably to their high-season revenues and helped the line. Cunard also took a hard look at their competition, particularly the highly successful ROTTERDAM (1959) of Holland–America, which had been designed both as a North Atlantic liner when the trade warranted and as a cruise ship in warmer waters when winter made the Atlantic inhospitable.

Sir John Brocklebank, chairman of Cunard, reluctantly announced on October 19, 1961, that the Cunard Line could not see its way clear to order

The 125th anniversary of the Cunard Line was commemorated with a special menu that surveyed the history and status of the fleet on July 4, 1965. Preparations were simultaneously being made for the laying of the keel plate of a giant new superliner at John Brown's on the Clyde.

the Q3. The plans for the 75,000-ton vessel were shelved forever because trading conditions could not justify replacing the QUEENS by similar tonnage, and it was back to the drawing boards. For over a year things looked grim, until it was announced in December 1962 that Cunard was deeply involved in plans for a smaller and more versatile liner. Details of the new design were provided by Sir John Brocklebank early in 1963. It was announced that the new ship would be around 55,000 tons and capable of transiting most of the major waterways of the world, such as the Panama and Suez Canals. It was to have a width of less than 110 feet and a length of less than 990 feet. In April 1963 it was announced that a decision was near on a new liner that would be totally revolutionary in design, rather than evolutionary as the QUEENS had been. By early summer 1963 plans for the ship were submitted to Marples at the ministry of transport once again. This time the government refused Cunard a special loan for the vessel, but did not completely close the door to aid. Instead, it was suggested that Cunard reapply for assistance to the new loan fund under the direction of Lord Piercy that had been established to aid shipowners willing to place contracts with British yards. Cunard promptly did so and received assurances of a loan of £17,600,000 toward the cost of the new liner.

Plans were sent to British yards interested in tendering for the ship on September 9, 1964. The earlier contract for the Q3 almost assuredly would have gone to a consortium led by Vickers-Swan Hunter of Tyneside, but this was not to be the case now. Strict attention to cost and delivery times was imperative for Cunard when the bids were received on November 30, 1964. The winner was announced within one month and the contract for the new liner was signed on December 30, 1964 with John Brown (Clydebank) Ltd., which had quoted both the lowest price and the earliest delivery date (May 1968). The ship was described in glowing terms as capable of holding her own on the North Atlantic and also as being one of the most fabulous resorts in the world. She could cruise anywhere and provide her passengers with a level of luxury unsurpassed by any competition.

The new ship was to cost £25,427,000, with an escalation clause to cover inflationary factors; £17,600,000 of the price was to be met by a government loan upon delivery of the vessel. However, Cunard had to find the money to pay the builders in order to receive substantial advance payment credits of some £4,000,000. There was no alternative but to mortgage the fleet. Accordingly, five liners and six cargo ships were mortgaged to a consortium of British banks to raise the money for the new ship. It was a difficult and dangerous time for the line, further complicated by the serious illness and subsequent retirement in November 1965 of Sir John Brocklebank as chairman. His successor was Sir Basil Smallpeice, an energetic and respected former general manager of BOAC.

The goal for the new ship was to create a vessel capable of presenting and selling to the public a whole new way of travel. There was no question

Captain William Eldon Warwick stands in front of his new command in December 1966 after seeing her for the first time at John Brown's on the Clyde. The launching date is nearly ten months away, but the 17,500 tons of steel plate in the hull already make it appear massive.

anymore of her being just a means of getting from point A to point B. Conditions in the travel industry had changed so drastically that to be successful the new liner had to be viewed as a floating luxury resort, a five-star hotel with the additional advantage of being able to go anywhere in the world. Happily for Cunard, the tremendous innovations in design, materials, and construction techniques in the 1950s and 1960s made possible the creation of a daring ship that could capture the attentions of the space-age traveling public.

July 2, 1965, was established as the day on which the first section of the keel would be laid at John Brown's on the Clyde for Yard No. 736. The berth to be used was the same from which the two earlier QUEEN liners had been launched. The welded steel section was in one gigantic section weighing 180 tons, 117 feet long, 23 feet wide, and 6 feet 3 inches high. In actuality, the initial unit involved three pieces welded together. When the first attempt was made to slide the 180-ton unit onto the greased oak blocks of the slipway, it had a mind of its own. The keel section refused to budge, but the cement anchor blocks began to lift out of the ground as the cranes took up the strain. Dry weather in western Scotland had played a trick on the Clydeside builders, and the keel-laying ceremony went ahead without the formal act itself. Subsequently the lifting and anchor equipment was reinforced and the 180-ton first section of the keel was moved into position on July 5, 1965, while the 125th anniversary celebration of the Cunard Line was still underway. Special menus graced the tables of diners the previous evening on the vessels of the fleet as the Cunard Line extolled the past and heralded the future with the keel laying of the new ship, No. 736.

Already publicists were eager for details of the giant new Cunarder. Certainly her machinery was going to be revolutionary, as she was to be the largest twin-screw ship in the world. Her three boilers were to produce superheated steam at 950 degrees Fahrenheit for turbines that would generate 110,000 shaft horsepower. All this was to be done on half of the fuel consumption of the old QUEENS. The electrical generators in the new liner were to create enough power to serve the needs of a city of over 20,000. The list of superlatives seemed to go on forever.

Extensive design work on the hull was carried out by the Cunard designers and by the National Physics Laboratory. Then the staff at John Brown's also put the hull form of the ship through test after test in the yard's restructured experimental tank and fed the results into a new IBM computer. The computer analyzed the statistics and fed back evaluations within an hour—a process that used to take weeks. Time was of the essence and a tight organization was crucial to the financial success of the project, from the standpoint of the builders and of the steamship line. John Rannie, managing director of John Brown, was a key individual in the process of overseeing the entire shipyard, but George Parker, shipyard director, was the individual who kept a tight watch on the actual building and ensured that materials were in

A 12-ton section of the aluminum superstructure of the ship is lifted into place. Approximately 130 sections like this one would make up the superstructure of the liner, and the weight saved would make it possible for her to have a draft 7 feet less than the old QUEENS.

By September 29, 1966, fifteen months after the keel laying, 9,500 tons of steel were in the hull lying on the building berth and 1,400 men were at work on the ship. The large stern frame weighing 62 tons was ready for positioning, and special sheer legs had to be positioned to lift the large casting that had been brought to the site by barge. The stern frame provides a secure housing for the rudder. (Photo courtesy of the John Maxtone-Graham Collection.)

place as required. Organization was greatly assisted by the ability of computers to keep track of the whereabouts and status of such things as the 100,000 different pieces of pipe the ship would need.

Cunard wanted to have their personal representative on the scene at John Brown's at the earliest possible opportunity. Accordingly, on December 7, 1966, at a management conference held in Winchester, where the head officers of the company and seventeen of the twenty-seven captains were present, it was announced that Captain William Eldon Warwick, relief captain of the QUEEN MARY and QUEEN ELIZABETH, was being appointed as master-designate of the new ship, effective immediately. Captain Warwick, a native of Birkenhead, was 54 at the time. He was the youngest captain ever to be appointed master of a QUEEN liner. He had been with the line for thirty years, joining Cunard as third officer of the LANCASTRIA in 1937.

Among the revolutionary aspects of the new Cunarder was the use of 1,100 tons of welded aluminum in the superstructure of the ship. So much of the light metal had never been used before in marine construction, but the advantages in stability and weight were enormous. This was also the first time that aluminum was to be an integral part of the stress-bearing hull of a ship. The development of complex and sophisticated alloys had brought the metal "of age," and the invention of the "inert-gas shielded metal arc (MIG) welding process" made possible both semi-automatic assembly and fast construction. The "state of the art" techniques developed and refined for the installation of the aluminum components on the new ship by Alcan Industries Limited were so advanced that representatives of the builders, the line, and Lloyds were invited to a series of seminars at Alcan's Banbury facilities in order to learn about the processes. The work target for the superstructure once erection began was 30–35 tons a week, and this allowed little room for delay. Since steel and aluminum will inter-react if they come into contact with each other, great care had to be taken to maintain the purity of the aluminum operations. To this end and the cement floors of the erection sheds were sealed with a special compound to eliminate any steel fragments or dust from previous construction, and heavy-duty industrial vacuum cleaners were constantly in use.

Looking at the construction of the new ship from a fabricating point of view, one can consider an all-welded superstructure, like an all-welded hull, as a single piece made up of a large number of subpieces. The sections were prewelded in the shipyard's shops and subsequently moved to the building berth for assembly in the ship. The lightness of aluminum allowed great freedom in the size of the prefabrications; the only limitation was due to the size of the doors through which they would have to pass to reach the building berth. These doors were 36 feet by 22 feet and could accommodate aluminum assemblies up to 12 tons. The result was that approximately 130 separate multi-ton pieces were welded together to create the superstructure of the new liner. Great care was taken with the attachment of the aluminum superstructure to the steel hull wherever the two metals might come into contact in order to avoid corrosion through electrolytic action. The firm of John S. Craig & Co. Ltd., Glasgow, developed a flexible epoxy liquid that was applied to one of the two surfaces after an elaborate cleaning and curing process. The two metals were riveted together, and in the heating process a tight seal was formed, prohibiting contact between the two metals and the intrusion of water into the joint.

By November 1966, when this picture was taken, 2,500 men were at work on the new Cunarder. The steelwork was up to the promenade deck, some 80 feet high. The John Brown Yard and Clydebank, Scotland, spread out in a panorama before the photographer working from one of the giant cranes. (Photo courtesy of the John Maxtone-Graham Collection.)

By April 1967 the huge hull of No. 736 soared 95 feet into the Clyde skyline. The assembly schedule called for the installation of 30–35 tons of steel and aluminum a week into the ship. (Photo courtesy of the John Maxtone-Graham Collection.)

The rudder of No. 736 weighs 70 tons and is 27 feet, 6 inches long and 23 feet, 6 inches deep. The surface area equals 482 square feet and the hinge pin alone is 7 feet high, 26 inches in diameter and weighs 5 tons. The rudder is filled with plastic foam to make it leakproof and to prevent internal corrosion. (Photo courtesy of the John Maxtone-Graham Collection.)

Four of the thirteen decks in the new ship are aluminum: the upper, boat, observation, and sports decks. These decks also include the two outdoor swimming pools toward the stern of the ship. Beneath the superstructure is the steel promenade deck, which was cleared and marked for the aluminum prefabricated units early in January 1967. The first unit of the upper deck was lowered into position on January 21. Within eighteen weeks the upper deck was well advanced, and within six months the superstructure clearly was emerging. When the aluminum superstructure was completed, the savings in weight to the new ship would give her a 7-foot reduction in draft over the older QUEENS, an incalculable asset in view of Cunard's desire to use the vessel extensively for cruising.

The main propulsion machinery was manufactured by John Brown Engineering (Clydebank) Ltd. and consisted of a twin-screw set of Brown-Pametrada turbines. Each unit would consist of a high-pressure and a low-pressure turbine driving a propeller shaft through double-reduction, double-helical, dual tandem gearing. At 174 revolutions per minute, the maximum output of the machinery was rated at 110,000 shaft horsepower, with the expectation that the normal service rating would be around 94,000 shaft horsepower, at which the highest level of efficiency would be achieved. The turbines were designed to receive steam at 800 pounds per square inch pressure and 940 degrees Fahrenheit. Among the cost-cutting economies made in order to bring the overall price of the ship down to what Cunard could afford was the deletion of an additional boiler from the specifications. The final contract called for three Foster-Wheeler E.S.D. II boilers, which also were built under license by John Brown. These were designed to produce 231,000 pounds of steam per hour under normal conditions and as much as 310,000 pounds at 850 pounds per square inch pressure and a working temperature of 950 degrees Fahrenheit.

The summer of 1967 sees the construction far advanced on No. 736 as the work force climbs toward 3,500. In this view from the Clyde River the majority of the superstructure has been assembled and the scaffolding has been removed on the port side.

A unique aspect of the new liner was the installation of a computer with a data-logging system. When the decision was made to see how much of the work of the liner could be handled by a computer system, negotiations were begun with the British Ship Research Association, resulting in equipping the ship with a Ferranti Argus 400 computer. A portion of the additional cost, regarded as experimental in nature, was underwritten by a grant from the National Research Development Corporation, with the understanding that if the unit proved commercially advantageous in practice, Cunard could buy it, and if not, the NRDC could remove it. Cunard assumed the obligation of making the knowledge it gained available to the shipping industry, and in the long run this would pay major dividends in automation, navigation, and fiscal control.

A major jolt in the proceedings occurred in July 1967 when John Brown informed Sir Basil Smallpeice that the cost of the new ship would probably be in the range of £28½ million, up some £3 million from the original contract price. Simultaneously Philip Bates, Cunard's managing director, came up with the bad news that there would be another £3½ million loss on the passenger ships in 1967. Smallpeice had no choice but to inform the Board of Trade, overseeing the building aid program, that the sum guaranteed to the line by the government was no longer adequate and that construction of the ship would have to cease unless additional resources could be made available. Complicating the issue was the fact that the announced launching day was September 20, 1967, and Her Majesty Queen Elizabeth II graciously had consented to launch the liner in the proud tradition of her grandmother, Queen Mary, and her mother, Queen Elizabeth, the Queen Mother. The Cunard board of directors met under tense conditions on September 14 as they awaited word as to whether or not the government would agree to increasing the loan. The situation was so critical that a negative response might force the board to cease operations and sell off the assets for whatever they might bring rather than lose more money. To the relief of everyone concerned, Harold Lever, financial secretary to the treasury, sent Sir Basil Smallpeice a note while the board was in session indicating that the government would increase the loan to Cunard from £17,600,000 to £24,000,000, permitting the launch of No. 736 to go forward as planned.

The rumors about the name for No. 736 were as numerous as they had been for the launching of the QUEEN MARY thirty years before. The old story was trotted out about Sir Percy Bates, then chairman of Cunard, and King George V discussing the name for the first QUEEN liner. Supposedly Sir Percy was thinking of the name QUEEN VICTORIA (with an IA name ending) when he asked the King for permission to name the new Cunarder after "our most illustrious Queen." The monarch responded that he would be delighted to ask Queen Mary when they returned to the Palace. That story almost assuredly is untrue, and many good authorities have tried to put it to rest. There would

Near to the launching day in September 1967 the two massive six-bladed propellers are installed. The rudder also is in place for the launch. The force of the propellers against the water as she goes down the ways will assist in slowing her momentum as she makes her bow to the world. Note the tiny figure of a workman beneath the 70-ton rudder; others are clustered near the port propeller. (Photo courtesy of the Frank O. Braynard Collection.)

not be even the possibility of such a problem this time. There was no question what Sir Basil Smallpeice and the Cunard Board desired, although there was the British tradition that only capital ships in the Royal Navy were named for sovereigns. The name was discussed with Lord Adeane, the Queen's private secretary, and it was decided simply to ask that the new ship be named QUEEN ELIZABETH, since by the time of her commissioning both of the earlier QUEENS would be withdrawn from service and she could assume the name vacated by one of her predecessors.

Launching day on the Clyde was pleasant, with good weather, as the crowds milled around the launching site or lined the river bank opposite to

Her Majesty Queen Elizabeth II has just named No. 736 the QUEEN ELIZABETH 2, on September 20, 1967, and the giant Cunarder rushes toward her element without a hitch in the proceedings.

a well designed attractive Tourist class there will be no need for the "Middle of the Road" passenger to look for anything beyond the Tourist class.

Law went on to discuss the fact that America had changed so much since World War II that the result was virtually a classless society wherein almost anyone in the vast middle segment could afford a substantial level of comfort.

Another telling argument was that as a three-class ship the QUEEN ELIZABETH 2 could accommodate between 1,860 and 2,000 passengers, depending upon the division of the three classes. As a two-class liner the new ship would be able to carry as many as 2,030 and, in spite of the increased payload, the number of staff needed would be less. Finally, under the direction of Sir Basil Smallpeice the two-class proponents won the debate because of the emphasis placed on cruising. The delay in the delivery schedule permitted this decision to be acted on carefully and thoughtfully.

The design team for the new liner was led by D. N. Wallace, chief naval architect for Cunard, whose life revolved around the new liner for nearly a decade before the launching. It was Dan Wallace who received the orders to change the ship from three to two classes when the hull was nearly completed, and it was Dan Wallace who made the philosophical statement that it was easier to redesign the ship with one fewer class than an additional one! Wallace received a vast amount of information from all over the world as hotels and liners were evaluated everywhere for ideas to make the new ship

The tugs rush to secure the liner before anything can go wrong in what has been a picture-perfect launch. (Photo courtesy of the Frank O. Braynard Collection.)

Safely secured in the fitting-out basin at John Brown's, the contours of the superstructure of the ship begin to take shape. By April 1968 the Signal Deck, Sports Deck, and Boat Deck are well underway, but no bridge, mast, or funnel is evident yet. (Photo courtesy of the Frank O. Braynard Collection.)

more efficient and more luxurious. The main requests for the new ship from all sources were the following: more single and two-bedded rooms linked with adjoining rooms; elimination of upper bunks whenever possible; more outside cabins with natural daylight: private showers, baths, and toilets in every cabin; ample wardrobe and drawer space; good lighting in the cabins; efficient sound insulation and absence of vibration; a wide range of public rooms so that passengers may enjoy communal entertainment in the nightclubs and theaters, or solitude and quietness in the card room, library, or reading room; greatly enlarged exterior deck space and swimming pools for cruising; and carefully planned, colorful, and stimulating facilities for children.

The two design coordinators were James Gardner for the exterior of the ship and Dennis Lennon for the interior layout and appointments. The basic challenge, as Gardner saw it, was how to make a good shape for a ship out of what could end up as a three-block-long set of floating apartment houses—exactly what many modern ships have become! The horizontal lines of the QUEEN ELIZABETH 2 were kept severely straight because curves cost space and money, yet, by a delicate balance of converging lines fore and aft, the optical illusion of subtle curves and grace was created. In fact, there is not a single curved plate in the sides of the hull. From bow to stern the desire was to keep the blustery North Atlantic winds away from passengers who may not always have rejoiced at the invigorating nature of deck chair travel. The funnel design of the QUEEN ELIZABETH 2 was dictated by the practical desire to ensure that the fumes and soot from the furnaces were carried well clear of the liner. When the model of the liner was fitted with a traditional funnel, the appearance was unsatisfactory and the exhaust gases from the engine room

Late spring 1968 sees the bridge in place, still minus its wings, and the funnel has been seated, but there is no mast. The name QUEEN ELIZABETH 2 is emblazoned on the hull with the uniquely modern designation that would make the QE2 famous.

simply rolled down the back of the funnel and smothered the broad open expanses of decks aft—a totally unacceptable result. Tailoring of wind scoops, exhaust pipes, and vents finally resulted in the upswept 67 foot 3 inch tall glory, towering a majestic $201\frac{1}{4}$ feet above the keel, the tallest funnel ever fitted on a QUEEN liner (the QUEEN MARY's were 59 feet and the QUEEN ELIZABETH's were 56 feet). The prominent mast forward did not have to be so massive, although it does serve as a wind scoop to carry kitchen fumes away, but it was created to complement the funnel and anything smaller could not carry off that design function. One of the greatest design challenges facing Gardner was the lifeboats, since, esthetically speaking, they mar the smooth lines of the ship. Nuances of color and design were combined in the color scheme of the lifeboats and their background in order to minimize their visual disruption of the clean lines of the ship. Initially the QUEEN ELIZABETH 2 was fitted with three bow anchors—port, starboard, and center—but a North Atlantic gale jammed the huge center anchor back into the bow and, following repairs, it was removed and stowed on deck as a spare. Reinforced steel plating covered the hole and strengthened the bow where the anchor had been.

Dennis Lennon, the joint coordinator for the QE2 with James Gardner, was responsible for coordinating the work of the ten-man team of top designers involved in styling the interiors of over 1,400 public rooms and cabins on the liner. Their design created a unified and integrated effect reflecting the best of contemporary style and manufacture Lennon's own team designed the restaurants, cocktail bars, a library, swimming pool, and all entrances, corridors, and staircases, as well as some of the cabins. Initially Dennis Lennon

One of the giant cranes is working through the turbine hatch aft of the funnel that descends directly to the engine room of the liner. Lifeboats are in place on the starboard side of the Boat Deck, and painting is underway. A dry cargo bulk carrier can be seen under construction behind the QUEEN.

had been brought into the consultation process on the new liner through the invitation of Lady Brocklebank, when Sir John Brocklebank had been chairman of Cunard. There had been some disgruntlement over such an important appointment without some sort of design competition. However, Lennon's achievements soon stifled all grumbling and made him one of the greatest successes of the Brocklebank period.

In addition to Lennon, Jon Bannenberg of Australia played a major role in fashioning the image of the QE2. Bannenberg designed a number of the premium-class cabins, a swimming pool, the card room, and the majestic panoramic Double Up–Double Down Room with its 20,000 square feet stretching the width of the liner and soaring through two decks. The main color schemes of red, silver, and clear glass have survived the test of time and made this one of the most successful public rooms on any liner afloat. The second-floor balcony area has gone through a number of transformations, but the room remains a remarkable utilization of space. David Hicks designed the initial tourist-class nightclub, the Q4 Room, and Michael Inchbald designed the quarterdeck library and the magnificent QUEENS Room, the principal first-class public room. Gaby Schreiber turned her considerable artistic skill to the creation of the largest theater afloat in the second of the two-deck-high public rooms of the ship. She also was responsible for the design of a series of suite rooms and the tour office. Stefan Buzas and his partner, Alan Irvine, were responsible for another nightclub, the 736 Club, a section of suites, the initial shops, and the boat deck gallery. Mrs. J. Pattrick undertook the decor of the officers' and crew's accommodation, as well as the hospital on the ship, with the goal of making all facilities as much as possible like a normal home in color and furnishings. It was fully realized that if the QUEEN ELIZABETH 2 was to go cruising a great deal, members of the crew would be serving extended periods of time away from Britain and that the off-duty areas of the ship should be made as attractive as possible. The partnership of Crosby/Fletcher/Forbes was responsible for all of the graphics on the ship so that all signs and public notices everywhere were in the same basic style. They also designed the splendid observation lounge, or Look Out Bar, across the front of the ship, which was one of the most popular facilities on the liner when commissioned. Professor Misha Black, professor of industrial design (engineering) at the Royal College of Art, who served as the coordinating architect for the public rooms in the P&O liner ORIANA, designed the synagogue for the QE2. Two students from the Royal College of Art, Elizabeth Beloe and Tony Heaton, were commissioned to produce the designs for the children's play area on the QUEEN ELIZABETH 2. In the future literally thousands of children were to enjoy this section of the liner, since it was not only a superbly stimulating center for young minds, but also included a miniature theater where cartoons and films were shown.

Significant of the change in philosophy in connection with the design and layout of the new ship was the desire to open as many of the public rooms as possible to a view of the sea. The attitude of the previous hundred years had been to make passengers crossing on a great transatlantic liner forget that they were at sea. Opulent public rooms gave the illusion of "life as usual" with the assumption that one might never have left port. When ships were the only means of crossing the ocean, the trip was often dreaded as much as appreciated; therefore, it was appropriate to camouflage the fact that the passenger was at sea. Millionaires could feel as comfortable in the great public rooms and suites of the AQUITANIA as in their own homes. It was possible, of course, to go out on deck, but it was desirable for only a few months of the year and even then was an invigorating, and for some unpleasant, experience. In contrast, the design team for the QUEEN ELIZABETH 2 was actively encouraged to emphasize the sea. The passengers who traveled by transatlantic liners, Cunard reasoned, did so by choice rather than lack of alternatives. Hence the great restaurants of the liner were placed high in the ship so that passengers dining on gourmet cuisine could have the best of both worlds: a grand hotel and an ocean vacation. Furthermore, the basic nature of

A brilliant day on the Clyde shows the fitting-out basin at John Brown's, with the QE2 nearing completion. Paint crews are at work on the port side and the ship looks remarkably complete, although there still is no mast forward.

the new liner was to be an "open ship" operating without class distinctions whenever she was cruising but with regard for them on the North Atlantic. Eliteness would be available through cabin selection and restaurant assignment for those who desired it. The overall expenditure for interior design work and outfitting ways about £3,000,000 ($8,400,000), but, as Lennon said, "the public judge a ship by what has been done to the interior." The desire was to make the QE2 second to none.

The interim report of the Cunard Line for the half-year ending June 30, 1968, was the most encouraging news that Sir Basil Smallpeice, or any Cunard chairman for a decade, had been able to offer the employees and stockholders of the line. The slimming down of the passenger fleet by the removal from service and sale of the QUEEN MARY, CARONIA, CARINTHIA, and SYLVANIA had resulted in a profit of £2,576,000 on a total passenger and freight revenue of £24,565,000. In contrast, the interim figures for the previous year had shown a net loss of £2,031,000 for an actual turnaround of £3.1 million! The high prices brought by the Cunard tonnage that had been disposed of also made it possible for the company to inform the British government that it would not need the remaining £4 million of the £24 million loan made available to them in September 1967. It appeared that Cunard had instituted the twin management policies of rationalization of the passenger fleet and diversification of the firm's resources just in the nick of time. As a result of the profit posted, the board recommended a $7\frac{1}{2}$% dividend for 1968 up from the minimum of 5%, which in a number of previous years had had to be paid out of reserves instead of from profits. The financial position of the company was turned around even if there was still an enormous debt to service for the new ship. The future suddenly seemed very encouraging.

The "Q4" plans in a cutaway were available at the time of the launch on September 20, 1967, but, of course, no name could be attached to them; hence she could only be described as "the new 58,000-ton Cunarder." Later it would be realized that the QUEEN ELIZABETH 2 would weigh in at well over 65,000 tons, which would create some cause for concern until assurances were given that this would not curtail the range of her potential employment.

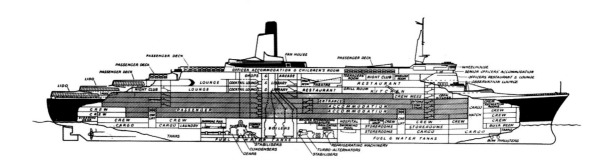

The fitting out of the ship went on as rapidly as possible, with an army of some 3,000 Scottish workers employed on the project at the actual building sight. By the time of the launch 17,500 tons of steel from Colvilles of Glasgow worth more than £1,000,000 ($3,000,000) had been used; so also had £500,000 ($1,400,000) worth of aluminum from Alcan; generators and other electrical equipment ordered from AEI were worth another £500,000; and air-conditioning equipment from Carrier capable of withstanding tropical sunshine was worth another £750,000 ($2,100,000). So the bills grew space with the ship.

Considerable attention was paid to suggestions aimed at making travel more of a pleasure for handicapped passengers. A percentage of the QE2's cabins were outfitted with bathrooms with lowered sills, larger doors, and plenty of swing room so that passengers traveling in wheelchairs could enjoy absolute mobility. Elevators also were adapted for handicapped passengers, and all public rooms, even if their main entrance was raised, such as the Columbia Restaurant, had convenient side entrances that were level.

A critical desire of Cunard was to have the QUEEN ELIZABETH 2 delivered on time so that the maximum advantage could be made of advanced scheduling and publicity. As early as December 1966 it appeared obvious that the liner would not be completely finished in time for the spring–summer 1968 season, and plans for that were scrapped. In determining the precommissioning schedule the two most critical problems were how much loading of stores on the ship could be done at the shipyard prior to delivery of Southampton, and how long of a trial period would be required at sea after the ship's delivery (with guests on board but no fare-paying passengers) before the ship could begin commercial service. The hotel department, in particular, was concerned that all furnishings be placed on board before leaving the shipyard so that nothing would be lacking. Furthermore, a catering storing period spread over some three months was regarded as imperative before leaving the shipyard. The hotel department also felt that two 8-day cruises with company guests should be undertaken in order to get all systems fully operational. Each section of the passenger accommodations was to be locked and secured as soon as it was finished.

The technical director, Thomas Kameen, led a team of seven Cunard engineers responsible for coordinating the design of the main turbines and auxiliary power plant, as well as all other main and minor machinery, including generators, evaporators, and the computer. Foremost among Kameen's concerns was the operation of the sprinkler system, since more vessels have been lost from fires in yards and while fitting out than probably from any other single cause. The technical commissioning program was started nine months before the ship left John Brown's, and included trials of all the major machinery as soon as possible. A proper sea trial had to include sufficient time to equal one North Atlantic round-trip voyage and take the ship into hot and humid weather so that the air-conditioning could be adjusted—a major problem on any new ship destined to operate both on the North Atlantic and in tropical waters. Cunard was under no delusions that the two week shakedown cruise probably would produce a list of adjustments and defects requiring an additional two weeks in port before acceptance. The goal in December 1966 was to have the QUEEN ELIZABETH 2 ready for commercial service by January 1969.

In the period between December 1966 and May 1968 the financial collapse of the Clydebank shipyards occurred and a new organization known as Upper Clyde Shipbuilders Ltd. was created to salvage whatever might prove economically viable. The projected £2,400,000 loss of John Brown and Company, Ltd., on the QUEEN ELIZABETH 2 was the final blow to that old firm, although the writing had been on the wall for some time. This placed Cunard in the position of finishing a ship with a different firm from that which had contracted for the vessel. The instability of the times also produced substantial labor unrest, which did not make life any easier for A. E. Hepper, chairman of Upper Clyde Shipbuilders, as he tried to honor deadlines. In fact, Upper Clyde signed a contract for a smaller passenger ship for Fred Olsen Lines largely because of the desire to guarantee some work after the QE2 left the yard and thereby maintain morale among the workers until the last great ship was safely delivered.

Sir Basil Smallpeice wrote to Hepper in May 1968 and emphasized the absolute necessity of maintaining the November delivery deadlines:

> I know full well that you are very anxious that the ship should be delivered on time because the publicity attached to the ship world-wide is such that a late delivery of it could not rebound on Upper Clyde Shipbuilders. As far as we are concerned, the revenue potential of the ship, even in the winter, is of the order of £$\frac{3}{4}$ million a month, and even four weeks delay would therefore be a very serious matter from our point of view, to say nothing of your own.

Cunard was willing to accommodate Upper Clyde in almost any way if the QUEEN just could get to sea on time! Upper Clyde responded by making John Rannie, local director of UCS, solely responsible for the QE2, with the power to do almost anything to get the ship ready for her trials. At the end of the summer Hepper set the tone for UCS by saying: "Although we are living in a very difficult situation at the moment, we are all very conscious of the extreme importance of this contract."

To the infinite relief of all concerned, just as dawn began to break over Scotland on November 19, 1968, the magnificent new QUEEN ELIZABETH 2 slowly eased her way out of the fitting-out birth at Clydebank and into the narrow river. Western Scotland had declared a holiday to watch the newest of the QUEENS majestically weave her way down the Clyde on a high tide. She needed all the water nature could supply, even if she did not draw as much as her predecessors. On the bridge was Captain William Warwick and, besides the normal complement of Cunard and Upper Clyde Shipbuilders personnel, Prince Charles, the heir to the throne. The trip downriver was not to be a long one, since the destination was the Greenock Dry Dock, barely 13 miles away. As the QUEEN ELIZABETH 2 completed her turn and prepared to move downstream, Captain Warwick fulfilled the fondest unspoken wish of the sixteen-year-old Prince when he asked his royal guest if he would like to blow the departure blast on the colossal horns of the liner. Prince Charles' eyes lit up, and he was clearly delighted to do so. Thus, the QUEEN's parting salute to her birthplace, where Her Majesty Queen Elizabeth II had launched her two years before, was given by the Prince of Wales. Nothing could have been more appropriate.

Once in the Greenock Dry Dock work on the completion of the QE2 appeared to slow. Five hundred carpenters were let go one week and one hundred hired back the next, generating instability in the work force while the accommodations on the ship remained a shambles. Since the workers could sail with her, after a week the QE2 left dry dock for her trials. The turbines steadily built up speed until she was racing along at 29½ knots, achieving this with two screws, whereas the older QUEENS had needed four, and with 50,000 horsepower less. The technical trials suddenly were interrupted by the discovery of an oil leak caused by a nonreturn valve that was contaminating the high-pressure steam system. There was no choice in the matter except to return to dry dock and completely clean the entire main and auxiliary steam circulating systems—a process that required the better part of two weeks. This delayed the resumption of the technical trials until the week before Christmas, and a holiday charity cruise for the benefit of the National Society for Cancer Relief was canceled. As a partial compensation to the Society, Cunard made a contribution to its treasury. When the sea trials were resumed, the QUEEN ELIZABETH 2 delighted everyone by reaching 32.46 knots at full speed with no sign of trouble.

Hurried arrangements were then made to take the ship on her final acceptance trials on December 23, with 500 members of the Cunard organization and their families along as "guests" and guinea pigs. Few "guinea pigs" ever ended up working so hard, since much of the passenger accommodation still required cleaning. Two hundred Clyde workers also went south with the ship in a desperate race to try to finish the most pressing carpentry work. Then, on the evening of December 24, as the liner steamed toward the Canary Islands, first the starboard high-pressure turbine and then the port turbine experienced problems. Initially the thought was that the rotor simply was imbalanced, but the fault was far more serious than that. Sir Basil Smallpeice, whose wife had been seriously ill, had missed sailing with the ship and he now flew out to Los Palmas with Anthony Hepper of Upper

The official visit of Her Majesty Queen Elizabeth II and His Royal Highness Prince Philip, Duke of Edinburgh, to the QUEEN ELIZABETH 2 occurred on the eve of the liner's maiden departure for New York, May 7, 1969. Captain William Warwick, master of the QE2, shows Her Majesty and Prince Philip around the bridge while Lord Mancroft, a Cunard director, and Sir Basil Smallpeice, Cunard managing director, look on. (Photo courtesy of the Collection of Mrs. Evelyn Warwick.)

Clyde Shipbuilders to inspect the situation. This was a time for Cunard to be very firm and, after hearing the extremely uncertain engineering report, as well as seeing the unfinished state of the passenger accommodations, Sir Basil announced that Cunard would refuse to accept the liner until everything was corrected.

The QUEEN ELIZABETH 2 slowly steamed back to Southampton to something less than a triumphant arrival and brought with her a load of publicity, since nearly 200 reporters had joined the ship in the Canary Islands for the trip back to England. However, the nature of the coverage was quite well balanced; most writers stressed the magnificence of the vessel, even if she was experiencing teething troubles. Very few complicated pieces of machinery do not require some adjustments and it is commonly forgotten that the QUEEN MARY had her share of problems after commissioning. (The considerable duplication of units in the QUEEN MARY's propulsion system made it possible to continue whatever the difficulty). The primary difficulty insofar as Cunard was concerned was to stimulate UCS to take immediate and drastic action to discover and solve the problem. By January 16, 1969, no positive identification of the turbine problem had been made and John Brown Engineering, the manufacturers of the turbines, was estimating at least another three weeks delay. On the face of that, Cunard canceled all future sailings. The company's position was very simple:

> Cunard cannot accept delivery until after the ship's turbines have been thoroughly re-tested and proved in further basin trials, speed trials and a prolonged acceptance trial under maintained pressure, followed by further inspection. It is impossible to say when this programme of correction, testing and proving of the ship's power plant can be completed.

The problem with the turbines may have been a blessing in disguise, because at least UCS could guarantee that during the next months the interior outfitting of the ship would be completed according to contract

Majestic and regal, the QUEEN ELIZABETH 2 entered service with her sailing from Southampton for New York. Her maiden appearance remained unchanged until late 1972.

terms by the end of January. Investigation revealed that some of the blades vibrated at unacceptable pitches until they shattered and spread havoc everywhere in their path. Various strengthening efforts were made that solved this crucial problem, and the turbines could be reconditioned. The result was a long, drawn-out process that did not near completion until mid-March. By March 16 it could be announced by a greatly relieved Anthony Hepper that the QUEEN ELIZABETH 2 would undergo basin tests alongside her Southampton pier and then go to sea for speed trials in the Channel. The Channel trials were a success at full power.

The QE2 went back into dry dock for cleaning and inspection, and then out on a shakedown cruise at the end of March during which all her machinery was given a workout, and finally the turbine casings were opened again for inspection. Everything being shipshape, or as Sir Basil put it, "Cunard-shape," the QUEEN ELIZABETH 2 finally was accepted by Cunard on April 20. Her final cost would be £29,091,000 ($69,818,400).

The acceptance on April 20 permitted a mini-cruise to the Canary Islands from Southampton on April 22, which actually marks the beginning of commercial service. Upon returning from the Canaries, the ship was reprovisioned for her maiden voyage and spruced up for a royal visit. On the eve of her first transatlantic crossing Her Majesty Queen Elizabeth II and Prince Philip renewed their association with the ship by visiting her for a royal tour. The visit heralded what Cunard was convinced would be the beginning of a brilliant career for Britain's largest liner. Captain William Warwick, master of the QE2, and staff captain George Smith received Her Majesty on board the ship. Among the ship's officers and heads of departments presented to the Queen were Donald Wilson, chief engineer; Jack Marland, deputy chief engineer; Mortimer Hehir, chief officer; James Smith, hotel manager; John Morton, deputy hotel manager; and Dr. William Deely, principal medical officer.

The Queen toured the bridge and the principal public rooms. The bust of Her Majesty, created by the sculptor Oscar Nemon, was in the Queen's Room. The Queen told of sitting for the sculptor on several occasions when he could not get the nature and position of the head to suit him and had unceremoniously wrenched it off. After the tour of the ship a luncheon was served in the elite Grill Room, with cold salmon as the main course washed down with a 1962 Montrachet wine from the substantial cellars of the liner. The visit of Her Majesty to the QUEEN ELIZABETH 2 maintained a Royal Family tradition of three generations.

On May 2, 1969, nearly five years after her keel laying and two years after her launching, the QUEEN ELIZABETH 2 sailed from Southampton with 1,400 passengers for Le Havre and New York on her maiden voyage. What had appeared on occasion to be the impossible dream had become a glorious reality.

CHAPTER THREE

A Royal Career

Docking in New York at the new North River passenger liner terminal is in some ways less challenging than at the old Cunard piers, but with any kind of a wind it still requires skill and practice to place the 963-foot QE2 in her slip.

The maiden Atlantic crossing of the QUEEN ELIZABETH 2 was an appropriate introduction to the solid comfortable luxury her passengers would enjoy in the future. The steaming time from Le Havre to the Ambrose light tower was 4 days, 16 hours, 35 minutes, which gave an average speed of 28.02 knots. Early on the morning of May 7 the QE2 was greeted by a flotilla of escorts as she neared the Verrazzano Bridge. She was led into the harbor by the U.S. Coast Guard cutter MORGENTHAU while the U.S. Navy destroyer CONWAY took up position astern. Mayor John V. Lindsay of New York and a party of dignitaries boarded the QE2 in the Lower Bay before noon, along with numerous members of the press. The basic feeling among those who came to greet her was that no vessel like her would ever be built again and that she represented the last of an era—the last great transatlantic liner. The gala parade up the harbor soon included hundreds of yachts and pleasure boats, as well as a chartered ferry boat. In New York tradition, the fireboats were present with their fire pumps spraying water high into the air. The day had started cool and overcast, but by noon the QUEEN ELIZABETH 2 was bathed in bright sunlight. She passed the Statue of Liberty and slowly steamed up the North River exchanging thunderous salute after salute with other vessels in the harbor. As the afternoon started to wane, the QE2 approached her berth at pier 92 and at 1512 hours "finished with engines" was rung. The maiden arrival of the QUEEN ELIZABETH 2 at New York had been one of the most spectacular welcoming celebrations that anyone could remember in the history of the port.

Many "arrival celebration" dinners were held all over New York City, as well as on the QUEEN . One thousand guests of Cunard Line at a supper dance enjoyed the amenities of the new ship and exchanged stories about her illustrious predecessors. The QE2 certainly was the biggest "happening" in New York, and those who came to see her were divided into two groups: those who had traveled on the old QUEENS and were astonished by the modern outlook of the new ship, and those who were social trend setters and were impressed that a ship could look so exciting. Among the guests were members of the diplomatic corps to the United Nations, including the ambassadors from Britain, France, Sweden, the Soviet Union, Ghana, and Morocco, and a generous selection of prominent men and women from industry, transportation, and finance. Other guests included Mrs. John V. Lindsey representing her husband, the mayor of New York, and the distinguished maritime author Walter Lord.

Many of the New York inaugural festivities on the QE2 took place in the huge "Double Room," which, with its red, orange, chrome, and glass color scheme, was strikingly different from anything in the old QUEENS. It was impossible for the guests to realize that the Double Room was the tourist-class public room when the ship operated with two classes on the North Atlantic. In assessing the new liner, one illustrious individual noted that it was characteristic of the times that there was virtually no noticeable difference between the first- and tourist-class public rooms. The subtle class distinctions were handled by a few discreet signs reserving areas for first class rather than the locked doors and barriers of previous vessels. The comments and reviews were mixed, but there was no question about the fact that the QUEEN ELIZABETH 2 both broke new ground and was strikingly different from everything that had gone before. If the QUEEN MARY in 1936 had been "evolutionary," there was no questioning the fact that the QUEEN ELIZABETH 2 in 1969 was "revolutionary." She therefore achieved exactly the effect that Sir Basil Smallpeice, Lord Mancroft, the directors of Cunard, and the ship's design team had desired: She was unique. As John Quinn of the *Daily News* summed up his story, "the old queens are gone. Long Live the Queen."

Passenger bookings steadily improved as the summer season began on the North Atlantic. When the QUEEN ELIZABETH 2 sailed from New York for her second eastbound crossing on May 22, she sailed with 1,650 passengers on board.

Upon arrival in Southampton on April 29, 1969, the QE2 had the pleasure of a second visit from His Royal Highness the Duke of Edinburgh. The purpose of the visit was to present the 1969 Council of Industrial Design awards. Among the 1969 winners were designers of the special dining room chairs created for the QUEEN ELIZABETH 2. While he was aboard, Prince Philip had a more thorough tour of the ship than he had on his previous visit. He was

The QUEEN ELIZABETH 2 makes her majestic entrance to New York Harbor for the first time on May 7, 1969. Coast Guard cutters, fireboats, tugs, ferries, and yachts escort her as she exchanges salutes with other vessels. The crossing from Southampton to New York was accomplished in 4 days, 16 hours, 35 minutes at an average speed of 28.02 knots.

Four hundred feet of liner in the slip and nearly six hundred feet to go. The QUEEN loses the Moran tug from her starboard side and the tug swiftly moves around the bow to a new position on the port side, where she can nudge the liner against the pier.

The QUEEN ELIZABETH 2 has just cleared the Verrazano Narrows Bridge on her maiden arrival in New York Harbor, and an armada has gathered to escort her to her berth.

shown some of the public rooms before being taken to the crew quarters, where he saw food being prepared for the crew mess. The tour also included the turbine control, engine, and boiler rooms.

The 1969 summer season passed relatively uneventfully, and the QUEEN carried an average of 1,550 passengers per crossing. The fortunes of the Cunard Line had begun to change for the better in 1968, even before the advent of the QE2, but now, with her increased earning capacity, everything began to look very promising indeed. The popularity of the QE2 among families traveling with young children grew steadily as it became known that the liner had some of the finest facilities and best-organized entertainment program ever created for children of all ages. By 1972 it was not unusual for the ship to be crossing with 200 to 300 children. Furthermore, if one was returning from a year or more in Europe with a family and did not want to restrict the baggage, the QUEEN could end up as a bargain over the airline surcharges for overweight luggage. The QUEEN earned for herself an enviable reputation as a spacious ship with comfortable accommodations and superb cuisine for all travelers.

As far as her qualities as a good sea ship, the QUEEN ELIZABETH 2 may well represent the ultimate achievement in naval architecture. The beautiful sheer lines of her hull below the waterline gave her a smooth entry into virtually any sea and resulted in the most stable performance of any of the great Atlantic liners. In addition, her stabilizers were designed and contoured precisely to complement the hull lines of the ship and were able to operate under virtually any sea conditions and considerably reduce rolling, even in severe weather.

Her seaworthiness was put to test in October 1969. The liner arrived in New York some ten hours late after having altered course several times during the North Atlantic crossing in order to avoid the worst of three major

storm systems over the ocean. In meteorological terms, a complex depression with associated storm winds ranging up to force 11 and accompanied by very heavy west-southwesterly swells caused a speed reduction and delayed arrival. On October 18/19 relief Captain F. J. Storey took the QUEEN over 100 miles south and again on October 20/21, when this action was repeated and accompanied by reduced speed in order to minimize passenger discomfort. When yet a third storm in the same depression was encountered less than 600 miles from New York, there was not too much the ship could do to make up the time with the 110,000 horsepower at her command. The official Cunard report stated: "Considering the magnitude of the storms, it was considered that QE2 made good headway and lived up to her reputation of being a good sea ship."

The news that the QUEEN had contributed £800,000 ($1,920,000) to the Cunard profits for 1969 certainly buoyed the satisfaction and expectations of the owners, since this represented less than a year's operations. Earlier, on October 18, 1969, it had been announced that before the QUEEN ELIZABETH 2 was nine months old Cunard would have repaid £2½ million of the government loans provided for the completion of the new liner and that they would be in a position to repay £500,000 every six months of the outstanding balance of £12 million. Sir Basil Smallpeice commented:

> The fact that we have been able to make these repayments is clear evidence of Cunard's all-around progress and growing cash flow. I am glad that we are able to show in this practical way that the Government's confidence in Cunard's new direction and management was not misplaced.

Additional good news followed on November 3, 1969, when it was announced that the Cunard Line had decided to invite tenders for one, and possibly two, new 1,000-passenger liners for the leisure market. While

On the maiden arrival of the QUEEN ELIZABETH 2 in New York three Moran tugs were in attendance just to make sure that everything went perfectly as the brand new liner gracefully turned into her slip and came up against the old Cunard Line piers.

preference would be given to British yards, shipbuilders from all over the continent were invited to tender for the ships, with Cunard reserving the right to make a selection on the basis of price, delivery date, and credit terms.

The plans for the 1969–1970 winter season were for the QUEEN ELIZABETH 2 to have a series of seven 10-day Caribbean cruises from New York. Wherever she went, the QE2 was given a royal welcome in a fabulous series of "maiden arrivals" that delighted passengers and islanders. In Kingston, Jamaica, the governor-general Sir Clifford Campbell and an official party were entertained on board while passengers were greeted by bands, mounted horseman, and a festival atmosphere on shore. The series of Caribbean cruises proved popular, although even the 28-knot speed with which the QUEEN rushed her passengers south could not eliminate the penetrating cold of a New York sailing.

When the QUEEN returned from the Caribbean on February 5, 1970, she encountered two problems: the New York tugboats were on strike and her pier was choked with ice. Captain W. E. Warwick had to ease his 963-foot ship steadily in and out of the slip four times in order to crunch the 6-inch ice flows with her 65,000 tons and then, with the aid of the bow thrusters, berth her alongside the pier. Afterward the captain turned to his officers and said: "I never thought we would have to use a £30 million ship as an ice breaker."

Personal tragedy occasionally affects the life of those who go to sea, and sometimes in a dramatic way. The first instance of a "man overboard" occurred on March 30, 1970, when the QUEEN ELIZABETH 2 was on passage from Barbados to Madeira. The ship was steaming along at 28 knots when at 1202 hours it was reported to the bridge that a man had been seen falling overboard. Immediately the speed was reduced and the rescue launch crew alerted. Within sixteen minutes QE2 had completed a "Williamson turn," a maneuver that brought the ship onto her reciprocal course. During the turn lookouts were scanning the area, and at 1249 hours an object was sighted floating in the water. Within five minutes the ship was stopped and the rescue launch was underway. At 1301 hours the body of a crew member was recovered from the sea, but efforts to revive him proved unsuccessful. The launch was recovered by 1316 hours and the ship resumed her passage. Although the incident was unfortunate, it did serve to demonstrate the maneuverability of one of the largest ships in the world.

By coincidence, it had been arranged for stop trials to be carried out the following week in the presence of British board of trade surveyors for the purpose of verifying and checking the ability of the ship to stop under emergency conditions. These "emergency stop trials" were undertaken on April 5, 1970, while on passage from Lisbon to Le Havre. At 0918 hours the QUEEN was steaming through the ocean at 29.5 knots when the full astern order was given. Within 4 minutes at 0922 hours the forward momentum of the ship had been reduced to 8½ knots and both engines were moving astern.

Outward bound from New York, the QE2 passes the Statue of Liberty and heads toward the Verrazano Narrows Bridge. Passengers traveling on her for the first time always are convinced that the towering mast and funnel will not clear the underdeck of the bridge. Several feet of clearance do exist even at high tide.

By 0924 hours and ½ minute, 6½ minutes following "full astern," the QUEEN had stopped dead in the water and, within an additional 2 minutes, at 0926 hour and ½ minute, she was making 4½ knots astern. From full ahead at 29½ knots to full astern at 4½ knots in 8½ minutes!

The hospital facilities on the QUEEN ELIZABETH 2 are the largest and most modern ever provided on a commercial vessel. The team of doctors and nurses is capable of handling virtually any situation. Sometimes their services are in demand from other ships, as was the case on a number of occasions during 1970.

The first such call was on June 26, 1970, when the QE2 was on an eastbound passage from New York to Le Havre. A message was received from the 3,514-ton German motor vessel ZOSMARR on a westbound passage to Boston requesting medical advice for a sick Spanish seaman, Jesus Ferreira. Radio contact was established with the master of the ZOSMARR and the QE2's principal medical officer, Dr. W. E. Deely, who, after hearing details of the illness, decided that the seaman's life could be in danger. The position of the ZOSMARR was plotted and a course was set to rendezvous with her. It was found that only an 8-degree deviation to the south was required and that the QE2 should meet the ZOSMARR shortly after midnight. At 2000 hours Captain William J. Law gave the order to steer the new course to close with the German ship, which was also instructed to steer a reciprocal course. While making for the rendezvous, the QE2 encountered dense fog, and her high definition radars remained constantly manned as they scanned ahead. At 2345 hours the radars picked up the ZOSMARR 18 miles away, exactly on schedule. Contact was again made with the ZOSMARR to give her instructions to enable the ships to maneuver together as close as possible. At 0025 hours the engines were stopped and, shortly after, a launch was underway with a doctor on board. Because of the dense fog and the pitch darkness, the QE2 had to guide her launch across to the German ship. This was accomplished by the officer of the watch looking at a radar screen and giving instructions to the launch by walkie-talkie. The ZOSMARR assisted by blowing her whistle periodically, and the launch sighted the little freighter at 0109 hours and soon thereafter went alongside. Fortunately there was only a slight swell, and the sick seaman was able to descend to the QE2's launch by climbing down the pilot ladder. The launch sped back to the liner, was hoisted aboard, and by 0126 hours the QUEEN ELIZABETH 2 had resumed her voyage to Le Havre at full speed. Following treatment, Jesus Ferreira made a full recovery.

Under similar circumstances, assistance was also rendered to seaman K. Hopner from the trawler HEINRICH KERN on July 27, 1970, while the ships were in mid-Atlantic.

On October 29, 1970, when on passage from Las Palmas to Dakar, the QUEEN ELIZABETH 2 diverted from course at 1236 hours to render assistance to an engineer officer injured on S.S. CERINTHUS of the Hadley Shipping

Few ports in the world are more highly regarded by cruise passengers than Charlotte Amalie, St. Thomas, Virgin Islands. As the Caribbean sun begins to set the bow of the QUEEN ELIZABETH 2 points toward the resort hotel of Frenchman's Reef in an exquisite setting.

Company, London. The fifth engineer, David R. G. Senior had suffered second-degree burns on the hands and face and was in critical need of expert medical assistance. The QUEEN reached the CERINTHUS at 1332 hours and the lifeboat was away by 1350 hours, returning with the patient by 1422 hours, after which the QE2 resumed full speed and the lucky man received the medical care his wounds required. Happily, he made a satisfactory recover.

In June 1970 the QUEEN made her fastest crossing to date, covering the distance from Cóbh, Ireland, to New York in 3 days, 20 hours, 42 minutes, at an average speed of 30.36 knots. Her reputation was growing. Evidence of the success of the QUEEN ELIZABETH 2 was in the eastbound crossing of July 23, 1970, when she carried her 75,000th passenger, who received a plaque in commemoration.

In October 1970 the QUEEN received a royal present of her own when Her Majesty Queen Elizabeth II presented portraits of herself and of Prince Philip to the officers' wardroom. The presentation at Southampton was made by Sir Basil Smallpeice on behalf of Her Majesty to the wardroom president chief officer T. D. Ridley. In the next decade Captain Ridley would have a distinguished career that would see him become captain of the QE2 and subsequently vice-president in the Cunard Line and the permanent general manager on the ship.

Cunard's decision to order additional passenger liners resulted in a partnership with Overseas National Airlines, which had ordered a 17,000-ton cruise ship from The Rotterdam Drydock Company. This arrangement enabled Cunard to take delivery of a new medium-sized liner by the summer of 1971 and a second vessel a year later. On July 15, 1970, the announcement was made that the line had acquired 100% ownership of the new vessels from ONA and that they would be owned and operated exclusively by Cunard. Sir Basil Smallpeice, commenting on the decision, said: "It underlines Cunard's determination to re-establish a modern and profitable passenger fleet at an early date." In November 1970 it was announced that the first of the new 17,000-ton liners would be named CUNARD ADVENTURER in line with the desire of the company to stress the cruise and leisure aspects of the 700-passenger vessels.

One of the most dramatic experiences of the QUEEN ELIZABETH 2 happened the night of January 8/9, 1971. The giant Cunarder under the command of Commodore W. E. Warwick was anchored off Castries, St. Lucia, on a Caribbean cruise when an SOS was received from the French liner ANTILLES stating that she had run aground and was on fire near the island of Mustique in the Grenadines. The distress signal was received at 1905 hours and it was possible for the QE2 to respond very quickly, as she was already preparing to sail for her next port of call. By 1954 hours the QUEEN had weighed anchor and was steaming at full speed to the rescue. In the meantime all departments on board were alerted to prepare for 500 survivors. Launch

Sir Basil Smallpeice, chairman of Cunard (1965–1971), presents to Douglas Ridley, chief officer and president of the officers' wardroom, the picture of Her Majesty Queen Elizabeth II that was a gift of the Queen to the ship in 1970. Looking on from the right is Commodore William Warwick, master of the QE2, and to the left is Captain Mortimer Hehir. Warwick, Hehir, and Ridley were all masters of the ship.

crews were mustered, gangway and scrambling nets were prepared, and volunteer parties of the QE2 Scuba Divers' Club stood by. The hospital was on the alert and in the hotel department chefs and waiters stood by to prepare and serve food and drink. Additional blankets were made available, cabins prepared, and a reception desk was set up near the gangway to allocate them to the rescued as they came aboard. A list was made of those passengers with special skills who offered their services and of those who volunteered to give up their cabins to any needy traveler. Since the QUEEN had only 1,000 passengers on board for the cruise, she had sufficient staterooms to accommodate the majority of the ANTILLES' passengers without inconveniencing many of her own.

A scene of awesome power and majesty: the QUEEN ELIZABETH 2 slices through North Atlantic swells during a crossing in August 1972. The penthouses have not been added yet, although work on them is underway; hence the QUEEN looks much as her original designers intended—sleek, modern, and powerful.

The QUEEN ELIZABETH 2 offers a magnificent panorama in this official Cunard Line photo of the liner taken while on trials in the English Channel. The open expanses of deck toward the stern have never been equalled in any other vessel.

Three and a half hours after sailing from St. Lucia the QUEEN ELIZABETH 2 reached the search area at 2230 hours. As she approached Mustique, the ANTILLES could be seen as a pulsating glow on the horizon, ablaze from stem to stern and with flames soaring over 100 feet into the Caribbean night. The passengers on the QE2 had a clear view of the ANTILLES as the QUEEN passed within a quarter of a mile of the stricken liner vividly marking the treacherous reef. The ANTILLES' captain apparently had wished to show the cruise passengers the beautiful sight of Mustique Island against a Caribbean sunset. The slightly different course took the ANTILLES toward an uncharted reef, and islanders tried to wave a warning. Hugo Money-Coutts also tried in vain to give warning from his private plane as he circled the ship. The ANTILLES steamed on until she struck the uncharted reef with such an impact that it caused fuel tanks to split open. Oil leaking into the engine room soon became ignited and attempts to contain the fire failed as it easily spread over the water in the flooded compartments. Passengers on the ANTILLES were ordered to their lifeboat stations. When the abandon ship order was given, they proceeded ashore in lifeboats to the islands of Mustique and Bequia. The master and some of the crew remained on board in an unsuccessful attempt to fight the fire.

The QUEEN ELIZABETH 2 spent one hour in the search area near the burning inferno of the French liner and then sailed on to Grand Bay, Mustique, to take on survivors. It appeared as though there may have been a high loss of life because of the number of different places and ships to which passengers and crew of the ANTILLES had gone. The master of the QE2 had in fact stated that anywhere from 50 to 100 individuals were unaccounted for, in response to an early request for news from the French line. The QE2 was joined by other liners in the rescue area, including the EMPRESS OF CANADA and the OCEANIC, which, along with other vessels, searched for further survivors. The U.S. Coast Guard center in San Juan, Puerto Rico, the port from which the ANTILLES' cruise had begun, was in continuous communication with the QE2, keeping abreast of the situation and ensuring that all possible assistance that could be used was available. In all, 635 individuals were transferred to safety from the ANTILLES: 501 to Mustique by lifeboat and life raft, 85 to the French ship SUFFREN, and 49 to the nearby island of Bequia.

At Mustique night conditions and a heavy swell made the transfer of survivors from the shore to the QE2 difficult; nevertheless, between 0130 and 0530 hours the QE2's launches moved back and forth between the island and the ship with the ANTILLES' passengers. By 0505 hour on January 9, Commodore Warwick was able to assure the French Line at Fort de France, Martinique, that everyone had been accounted for from the ANTILLES, but that, according to all reports and the assessment of the ANTILLES' purser, the French liner was a total loss. Having taken all on board from Mustique, the QE2 sailed at 0530 hours for Barbados, where French Line agents commenced preparations to receive the ANTILLES' passengers. By the time the QUEEN ELIZABETH 2 arrived at Barbados the wind was too strong for her to go alongside in the harbor, so she anchored in the bay off Bridgetown. To assist with the ferrying of passengers and survivors ashore, seamen and launches from the CARMANIA, which was also in port, were directed to assist the QE2, as most of her crew had been on duty all through the night.

French Line officials boarded soon after arrival to arrange for the care and transportation of all those who desired it. Eighty-five passengers elected to remain on the QUEEN for a portion of her Caribbean cruise. These included sixty-seven Venezuelans who found it more convenient to disembark at La Guaira, Venezuela, and thirteen Colombians and five Dutch who elected to stay on board until Curaçao, Netherlands Antilles. The passengers who boarded the SUFFREN were also brought to Barbados. Captain Raymond Kerverde, the master of the ANTILLES and the last man to leave the burning liner, and the forty-eight other seamen on the little island of Beguia were picked up by another French ship, POINTE ALLEGRE. To this day the burned-out hulk remains on the reef off Mustique.

Congratulatory messages soon began to flood into the radio room of the QUEEN ELIZABETH 2. Michael Noble, British minister for trade, on an official visit to Venezuela, sent the following to Commodore Warwick:

> I have much pleasure in sending you and all your officers, staff, crew and passengers hearty congratulations on your magnificent achievement in coming to the rescue of the passengers and crew of the S.S. ANTILLES. This was in the best traditions of British seamanship. I am glad that my presence in Venezuela makes it possible for me to send you these congratulations direct.

The U.S. Coast Guard radioed from San Juan: "Your cooperation in rendering assistance to the S.S. ANTILLES on 08 January 1971 is greatly appreciated and demonstrates the continuing high standards of the Merchant Marine in keeping with the best traditions of the sea. Thank you". Sir Basil Smallpeice radioed from London:

> Have received following message from President of the French Line; I want to thank you for the assistance which has been afforded to us by Cunard in the accident which struck our liner ANTILLES. Please convey to Captain of the QE2 our deep appreciation for taking on board passengers which our crew had evacuated and put on Mustique Island.

When the QUEEN ELIZABETH 2 arrived at La Guaira, the president of Venezuela personally tendered his congratulations and thanks to the master and crew for their part in the rescue.

The remainder of the 1970–1971 winter Caribbean cruise was relatively uneventful. But on March 15 the QE2 was called on another mercy mission, en

During the night of January 8-9, 1971, survivors of the French Line's ANTILLES board the QE2 from her launches after being transported from the island of Mustique following the wrecking and burning of the French liner on an uncharted reef.

route from New York to Aruba, to aid a seaman who had fallen from the mast of the Norwegian vessel BESNA. A launch was sent across from the QE2 to collect the seaman and he recovered from his injuries.

The highlight of the early spring 1971 season was the maiden arrival of the QUEEN ELIZABETH 2 at Bermuda on March 26, 1971. Maiden arrivals always generate enthusiasm, but Bermuda has a special place in the hearts of many North Americans, and the Bermudians reciprocate these warm emotions where cruise ships and American and Canadian tourists are concerned. The QE2 was too large to dock in Hamilton and had to anchor in the Great Sound.

Unfortunately, the financial situation of the Cunard Line deteriorated substantially during 1970 as a result of soaring costs. In Britain the president of the chamber of shipping noted increases at a pace far greater than for a generation or more. In Cunard's case, prices of fuel oil for ships increased by between 80 and 100% within one year, and other costs, such as seafarers' salaries and wages, port charges, baggage, and cargo handling, increased between 17 and 41% in a similar period. A total loss of £1.9 million was declared, which also included Cunard's associated companies.

The presence of an economic recession in the United States and a strong U.S. government publicity campaign aimed at encouraging Americans to stay at home had not helped Cunard revenues. However, the outlook for the QE2 in 1971 appeared more promising, with cruise bookings running at around 1,300 per cruise in comparison with around 1,150 the year before. This was an increase of 13% and meant that the QUEEN would operate above the break-even level for 1971.

The French liner ANTILLES (1952, 19,828 tons, 599 feet by 80 feet) John H. Shaum, Jr. Collection.

CHAPTER FOUR

A Year in the Life of the Queen

The QUEEN ELIZABETH 2 pays the highest toll of any vessel using the Panama Canal on the basis of her size and the nature of her "cargo" as a passenger ship. In the case of the QUEEN the fees exceed $90,000 per transit, but this is still a bargain compared to the cost of steaming 11,000 miles around South America. (Photo courtesy of David Barnicote.)

Traditionally, the year-long schedule of the QUEEN ELIZABETH 2 begins with the first Atlantic crossing of the regular season around the middle of April. Some individuals who do not like to fly will, in fact, arrange their departure from Europe or the United States to coincide with this event. By planning a schedule of approximately twenty-five to thirty Atlantic crossings, the QUEEN succeeds in filling her cabins for virtually every sailing. On the North Atlantic she is the last of the great steamships, and heiress to a tradition of service stretching back nearly 150 years.

The first crossing in April to New York may be a little early for the QUEEN ELIZABETH 2 to begin a series of Atlantic crossings; therefore it will not be unusual for her to take an eight- to ten-day Caribbean cruise from New York. Americans in April will be getting spring fever, and the thought of an early spring vacation to the Caribbean often will produce a good response. Returning to New York with a tanned clientele, the QUEEN will then take an eastbound crossing to Southampton with the first passengers of the summer migration.

Since Cunard remains the premier British-flag steamship line in the world and since the line is British owned, there is a desire to have a balanced program of cruises on both sides of the Atlantic. Hence a counterpart to any Caribbean offering will be a cruise to the Atlantic Isles (Canary Islands, or Azores) originating at Southampton. British and continental passengers will have the opportunity to enjoy the amenities of the largest British-flag liner as she seeks warmer waters on the eastern side of the Atlantic Ocean.

Upon returning to Southampton, the QUEEN ELIZABETH 2 will be ready to take another North Atlantic crossing, and within recent years this has been to Philadelphia direct, or via New York. The warm reception given the QUEEN by the residents of the Delaware Bay region has brought the liner back. In Philadelphia the QE2 has served as a focal point for numerous charity galas ever since her maiden arrival in 1982 marked the opening of the 300th anniversary celebrations of the city. Upon occasion, the QUEEN will take a brief three-day cruise to "nowhere" from Philadelphia and/or an eight-day Caribbean cruise. A return crossing from Philadelphia to Southampton will provide passengers with the rare opportunity to sail on a great liner down the Delaware. Again, for marketing purposes, this provides a sensible combination of cruises and Atlantic crossings for the early part of the season.

In Southampton an enthusiastic group of British and continental passengers may be waiting to board the QUEEN for a ten- to twelve-day Mediterranean cruise from the end of May through the first week in June. Upon return from the Mediterranean the North Atlantic season will swing into high gear and the QE2 will spend the month of June ferrying passengers between Southampton and New York as the summer avalanche of travelers in both directions begins in earnest. A party cruise from New York may break the schedule in an effort to introduce more people to the ship on a less expensive itinerary and entice them to make bookings for longer cruises or a transatlantic crossing at a later date.

One mid-summer sailing that always is popular is the North Cape cruise from Southampton to the "Land of the Midnight Sun" and the fjords of Norway. The North Cape cruise nearly always features the natural magnificence of the Geiranger Fjord along with a visit to the land of the Lapps and reindeer, and occupies ten to twelve days during the latter part of July. Because of the tremendously long and varied coastline of Norway, the QUEEN actually has visited more different ports (thirteen) in that Scandinavian country than any other nation around the world. Following the North Cape will occur one to three North Atlantic crossings and then a cruise to the great natural fjord of the North American Atlantic Coast—the Saint Lawrence River—and Canada. The annual Canadian cruise to cooler climes always is popular and may include calls at Bermuda, one or more Canadian ports, and a majestic arrival at Quebec.

Atlantic crossings will finish out the month of August. Cunard, in planning the schedule of the QUEEN ELIZABETH 2, takes note of the fact that the American summer holidays traditionally end with the American Labor Day, early in September. The British summer holidays usually wind up near the end of September; hence, a party cruise from Southampton is appropriate in September to introduce more passengers to the amenities of the QUEEN there. With the genuine growth of a Philadelphia market, a fall transatlantic may well call in at the Delaware port as well as New York. September will see the winding down of the summer season. Perhaps it will be possible to slip in a short cruise from New York to Bermuda before returning to Southampton around October 1 and another longer cruise to the Mediterranean. A couple

At Martinique a native fisherman steers his boat by some of the Cunard launches that have brought passengers ashore from the QUEEN ELIZABETH 2 in the morning and now ride at anchor awaiting the afternoon rush to return to the ship.

The QUEEN ELIZABETH 2 has visited more ports along the long Norwegian coastline than in any other country. The annual North Cape cruise to the Land of the Midnight Sun always proves popular. One of the highlights of this cruise is the transversing of the Geiranger Fjord, with some of the most magnificent and rugged scenery in the world.

73

The QE2's launch speeds away from the pier at Charlotte Amalie, St. Thomas, Virgin Islands, with another load of passengers returning to the ship at the end of a full day.

Anchored off the Caribbean paradise of Martinique, the QE2 dwarfs local yachts.

more transatlantics, and by mid-October emphasis definitely will switch from the Atlantic to cruising as the weather makes warmer climes more attractive. An Iberian cruise may interest European customers in enjoying both the QUEEN and one of the favorite European playgrounds.

Boston, the "mother city" for Cunard in the United States, cannot be overlooked during any scheduling for the QUEEN ELIZABETH 2. Accordingly, a November crossing frequently will terminate in Boston in order that a cruise from New England to the Caribbean can occur. This may or may not include a call at New York going to or from the Caribbean. During the first two weeks in December the QUEEN will have earned her annual overhaul as she slips into a dry dock for a frantic period of adjustments and improvements and a paint job. After she emerges from her refit, there will be a positioning voyage to New York, which is the last North Atlantic crossing of the year, bringing Americans home for Christmas and the holidays.

Two fabulous Caribbean cruises for Christmas and New Year's will wind up the annual offerings to the Caribbean. The ship is decorated from stem to stern for the holidays and a traditional festive atmosphere accompanies the opportunity for the celebration of Christmas and New Year's in a tropical setting. When the QUEEN returns to New York around the middle of January, preparations will be ready for the longest and most fabulous cruise of the year—the Great World Cruise.

The world cruise, or its equivalent in time, the Great Pacific Cruise, provides useful employment for the QUEEN ELIZABETH 2 during nearly three months of the year. Among the highlights of the annual world cruise are a number of inaugural arrivals at places. Each new port or place puts on a show to greet the giant liner and her passengers with flower-bedecked native catamarans or mighty fireboats shooting streams of water high into the air. The spectacle always is exciting.

In the midst of the world cruise the QE2 sponsors a "Summer Festival," or "Fête," that breaks one of the longer segments between ports and serves to raise money for charity. All the hoopla and festivities of a normal summer festival are included, such as a kissing booth, a tug-of-war contest, raffles, "Tombola," "A Human Fruit Machine," and a drawing for a date with the "prettiest girl on the ship." Everyone becomes involved in the light-hearted frivolity for a good cause.

Whenever the liner crosses one of the great demarcation lines of the globe, appropriate ceremonies also occur, with selected individuals representing everyone in whatever "Father Neptune" at his most awesome and hilarious commands.

One of the most fabulous experiences in the QUEEN's itinerary each year is a transit of the Panama Canal. Frequently this segment of the world cruise is booked to capacity, with a waiting list of impatient travelers desiring the experience of crossing from the Atlantic to the Pacific on the largest liner

One of the great cruises of the QUEEN ELIZABETH 2 nearly every year is the Canada and Atlantic Isles cruise. A frequent high point of this trip is the visit to Quebec, where the QUEEN now docks in the shadow of the Plains of Abraham and the Chateau Frontenac (August 1983).

One of the most dramatic experiences a cruise or an Atlantic crossing can offer is a night sailing. These do not occur too often, but when they do the QUEEN ELIZABETH 2 is a dramatic sight as she slowly backs out into the North River, with all her lights ablaze and enough electricity being expended to supply a city of 20,000.

The QUEEN slowly moves in toward the new quay adjacent to the Old Town of Quebec, which was founded by the French and dates back to the early seventeenth century. The docking operation against the current of the mighty Saint Lawrence must be handled with care. (Photo courtesy of James MacLachlan.)

The pair of Miraflores locks marks the beginning of any transit of the Panama Canal from the Pacific side.

The size of the QE2 makes any transit of the canal an adventure; the maximum clearance is only 30 inches per side. The liner is 963 feet in length and the locks are 1,100 feet.

The Pedro Miquel lock was built somewhat inland from the Miraflores locks on the Pacific side as a defense measure. This was done before the advent of the airplane and when a distance of 20 miles was considered beyond the range of big gun warships. The Panama Canal formally opened for business in August 1914.

The QUEEN ELIZABETH 2 steams through the Gaillard Cut 85 feet above sea level and over the Continental Divide. All rainfall falling on the land to her stern flows into one ocean and all that at her bow flows into the other. Over 25,000 men lost their lives building the Panama Railroad (1849–1855) and then digging the Panama Canal (French effort, 1878–1888, and American effort, 1903–1914). A small stone memorial at the Continental Divide commemorates their sacrifice. (Photo courtesy of David Barnicote.)

above:

She approaches a lock a small rowboat comes out to greet her and take the first of the lines from the liner to the mechanical "mules" waiting to pull her through the lock. The Panama Canal is the only waterway in the world where the pilot assumes responsibility for the vessel. If anything goes wrong, it is the fault of the Panama Canal Company.

There are only inches to spare as the QUEEN slips into a lock. The electrically powered cog-railroad "mules" pull the huge liner through the locks in tandem.

After leaving the Gaillard Cut, the QE2 crosses Gatun Lake, one of the largest man-made freshwater lakes in the world, in order to reach the Gatun locks on the Atlantic (Caribbean) side of the isthmus. (Photo courtesy of David Barnicote.)

Twenty-six million gallons of fresh water from Gatun lake supply the power through gravity flow to move the Queen through the locks. No pumps are necessary.

As the lock gates open, the QUEEN prepares to continue her voyage.

The three Gatun Locks on the Atlantic side are all together and are not divided like the Pacific trio. In any crossing from the Atlantic to the Pacific passengers marvel at the wonders of the Panama Canal locks.

ever built capable of the feat. The six locks that comprise the mechanical portions of the Panama Canal are 110 feet wide by 1,000 feet long. The QUEEN ELIZABETH 2 is 105 feet wide and 963 feet long. Hence, when the QUEEN leaves the Caribbean and steams past Cristobál toward the Gatun locks, the impression is that she never will succeed in "threading the needle." Slowly but surely, the huge liner edges into the first of the three locks at Gatun that will lift the ship 85 feet above the Caribbean to the level of Gatun Lake, which spans the continent. Once she is locked in, the clearance on each side will be less than 30 inches in a skintight fit. Then 26,000,000 gallons of water will begin to flood into the first of the Gatun locks by gravity feed to lift the liner. The easiest way to think of the process is to visualize an elevator serving three floors that lifts the ship from one to the next until the QE2 reaches the giant 134-mile-long freshwater body that is Gatun Lake. Several hours' steaming will be necessary to cross the 30-mile-wide lake, including a passage through the picturesque Gaillard Cut, where the canal was dug through the mountains of the Continental Divide. A monument marks the Continental Divide and is a memorial to those who lost their lives building the waterway.

On the Pacific side of the isthmus, the QUEEN approaches the Pedro Miquel lock, which is the first of the three leading from Gatun Lake to the ocean. The Pacific Division locks are separated slightly by Miraflores Lake. This was done in order to provide greater protection from the guns of potential enemy warships. A brief passage through the Miraflores Lake brings the QE2 to the last pair of locks, the Miraflores locks, which lower the ship the remaining distance to the Pacific Ocean. Transit time for the Panama Canal ranges from 6½ to 10 hours, and for passenger liners, like the QE2, and other vessels whose schedules are critical, an advanced reservation system is permitted guaranteeing a priority transit of the waterway. The transit fees for the Panama Canal are based upon the tonnage of the vessel as calculated by the Canal Authority, and the QUEEN ELIZABETH 2 pays the highest sum of any vessel when she uses the shortcut across the Isthmus. In 1984 the transit costs for the Panama Canal were over $90,000. Yet the savings over the 11,000-mile trip around South America are so great that the transit fees actually represent a bargain in operating costs, let alone convenience.

All voyages on the QUEEN ELIZABETH 2 can be tailored to suit individual preferences or time parameters. Today's marketing, aided by the speed of jet aircraft and the accessibility of virtually any major seaport in the world to air travel, makes it possible for passengers to experience the whole of a world cruise, if they have the time and inclination, or to enjoy sections of the cruise, with swift air service to and from the QUEEN, wherever she may be. In 1984 it was possible to fly out and join the liner at a variety of destinations and enjoy segments of the world cruise from two weeks to three months.

Arrangements also can be made to connect with other ships in the Cunard

San Francisco is one of the most magnificent natural harbors in the world. The passage under the Golden Gate Bridge heralds the arrival of the QUEEN in one of the most cosmopolitan cities in the world.

fleet: the CUNARD COUNTESS in the Caribbean, or the CUNARD PRINCESS on the Mexican Riviera or Alaska, or the two recent acquisitions from Norwegian American Cruises, the SAGAFJORD and the VISTAFJORD. For those who like to spend more time ashore, Cunard offers the fabulous resorts of Paradise Beach in Barbados and La Toc Hotel on the island of St. Lucia. Cunard also owns the world-famous Ritz Hotel in London and other first-class hotels in Britain.

Throughout the year on board the QUEEN ELIZABETH 2 activities are available to fulfill every individual mood or need. Each voyage there is a team of expert lectures on board. Guest speakers and famous personalities give talks about their lives, professions, or experiences. These have included Dr. Christiaan Barnard, Percy Thrower, Helen Gurley Brown, Ruby Keeler, Scott Carpenter, Sir Edmund Hillary, Jackie Stewart, Larry Hagman, Lillian Gish, Vic Damone, Dr. Norman Vincent Peale, Vidal Sassoon, and Liv Ullman, to name only a few.

Those who prefer competition can enjoy an abundance of games and tournaments. Bridge is always popular, and an expert is on hand to help you improve your game. There is a professional golfer with the ship on every voyage, and a golf-driving range and putting course on deck. Paddle tennis, table tennis, and trap-shooting facilities are available, as well as traditional shipboard activities like shuffleboard, bingo, "horse racing," and guessing the daily "tote," or ship's daily mileage. To many weary travelers the greatest

A scene of splendor as the majestic QUEEN ELIZABETH 2 slowly steams up the channel toward Southampton with all her lights ablaze and a low cloud ceiling reflecting them back on the ship. The picture was taken from the NIEUW AMSTERDAM late on the evening of June 30, 1970, as the two passed "like ships in the night."

luxury simply is to do nothing for a while until one has recouped, to seek out a peaceful spot somewhere on the great open decks or a comfortable armchair in one of the many rooms.

A varied program of entertainment is a nightly occurrence on board, from singers, magicians, and dancers to classical concerts and performances by world-famous artists. Somewhere in the ship one of the dance bands will be playing, providing a variety of tempos, and the disco is often active into the small hours of the mornings.

Many thousands of words have been written about food and dining on board the QUEEN, culminating in a recently published book by Carole Wright, *The Cunard Cookbook*. However, words cannot fully describe the gastronomic experience of a voyage on the QUEEN ELIZABETH 2—it has to be lived to be understood. *Holiday* magazine described the meals on the ship as "one of life's most memorable gastatory extravagances."

The provisioning of the ship for a North Atlantic voyage will involve such varied items as 25,000 pounds of beef, 22,000 pounds of fresh fruit, 150 pounds of caviar, 600 jars of baby food—and 50 pounds of dog biscuits. Within the stores on the QUEEN will also be found forty-one brands of whisky and forty-three brands of cigarettes. On a normal transatlantic round trip the ship would carry, on average, the following:

The Souls Sheet provides the fundamental breakdown of passengers, officers, and crew for any voyage. The enormous carrying capacity of the QUEEN ELIZABETH 2 is dramatically underlined with the simple figures: passengers, 1,653; officers, 86; crew, 830; total souls = 2,569. Furthermore, while Voyage No. 93 (west) in August 1972 was well booked, she could, if necessary, accommodate nearly 400 additional passengers and almost another 100 crew.

FOOD

Biscuits	2,000 lb	Eggs	220 cases
Flour	3,000 lb		(360 per case)
Cereals	800 lb	Cream	3,000 quarts
Rice and other		Milk	2,500 gallons
grains	3,000 lb	Fish	1,400 lb
Tinned fish	1,500 cans	Lobsters	1,500 lb
Canned fruit	1,500 gallons	Crabs	800 lb
Herbs, spices	50 lb	Fresh fruit	22,000 lb
Jam, marmalade	700 lb (bulk)	Frozen fruit	2,500 lb
Jam, marmalade	800 dozen jars	Ice cream	5,000 lb
Juices	3,000 gallons	Kosher food	600 lb
Tea bags	50,000	Beef	25,000 lb
Tea (loose)	500 lb	Lamb	6,500 lb
Coffee	2,000 lb	Pork	4,000 lb
Sugar	5,000 lb	Veal	2,000 lb
Baby Food	600 jars	Sausages	2,000 lb
Dog biscuits	50 lb	Chicken	5,000 lb
Caviar	150 lb	Duck	3,000 lb
Foie gras	100 lb	Turkey	5,000 lb
Butter	3,500 lb	Fresh vegetables	27,000 lb
Bacon	2,500 lb	Potatoes	300 cwt
Ham	1,200 lb	Pickles, sauces, and	
Cheeses	3,000 lb	condiments	2,000 bottles

BAR STORES

The bars on the QUEEN ELIZABETH 2 consume the following from stores and a wine cellar that boasts 25,000 bottles:

Champagnes	1,000 bottles
Assorted wines	1,200 bottles
Whisky	1,000 bottles (29 Scotch, 8 American, 2 Canadian, 2 Irish)
Gin	600 bottles (7 brands)
Rum	240 bottles (5 brands)
Vodka	120 bottles (3 brands)
Brandy	240 bottles (10 brands)
Liqueurs	360 bottles (18 types)
Sherry	240 bottles (5 brands)
Port	120 bottles (4 brands)
Beer	12,000 bottles plus 6,000 gallons
Cigars	4,000 (18 brands)
Cigarettes	25,000 packs of 20 (19 British, 20 American, 1 French, 2 Egyptian, 1 Russian, 1 Turkish)
Tobacco	100 lb (9 British, 5 American)
Duty-free packs	1,000 26-ounce bottles of spirits, 1,000 32-ounce bottles of spirits

From one of the QE2's launches looking up the top of the funnel towers 169 feet, 1 inch above sea level. The funnel is painted in the traditional Cunard colors used since August 1982.

An automobile is swung out of the hold of the QUEEN ELIZABETH 2 shortly after the liner's arrival in New York. If the tide is right and there are not too many cars, they can be driven on and off the ship by ramps. Courtesy Deborah Flayhart.

The massive bow of the QUEEN ELIZABETH 2 looms over the surrounding sea in this view taken while the ship was at anchor off Newport, Rhode Island, on a cruise.

The bridge of the QUEEN ELIZABETH 2 is the nerve center of the ship. An officer is on duty here 24 hours a day when the ship is in port, and there are two or more officers when the ship is at sea. Automatic navigation equipment and radar keep the ship on a safe course.

The towering mast of the QUEEN was designed to complement the funnel and serves a variety of purposes, from communications to kitchen exhaust. The flags flying from the mast in this instance (left to right) honor the country being visited, the island of St. Lucia, convey the information that the ship is about to sail, and indicate the country of registry (Great Britain).

LINENS

The linen consumption of the QUEEN ELIZABETH 2 during a normal transatlantic round trip is staggering (today the laundry is run under a concession to a firm employing Chinese):

Tablecloths	5,864
Blankets	8,600
Oven cloths	2,000
Sheets	23,200
Pillow cases	26,200
Laundry bags	6,500
Bath mats	3,300
Hand towels	31,000
Bath and other towels	26,000
Glass and waiter's towels	14,000
Aprons	3,000
Deck rugs	1,500

GLASSWARE, CUTLERY, AND CROCKERY

No great kitchen operates without an enormous supply of eating and serving pieces of all nature. The QUEEN is not exception and carries the following:

Glassware	51,000	items
Crockery (dishes)	64,000	items
Kosher crockery (dishes)	3,640	items
Cutlery	35,850	items
Kitchenware	7,921	items
Tableware, including condiment sets, serving trays and a variety of other pieces in silver and stainless steel	64,531	items

The builder's plate of the QUEEN ELIZABETH 2 makes note of the changes that occurred in Scottish shipbuilding in the 1960s. The contract for the ship was signed by John Brown & Co. (Clydebank) Ltd. in 1964, but its bankruptcy and the rationalization of shipbuilding in Western Scotland ultimately brought a number of yards together under the name Upper Clyde Shipbuilders Limited, which was the firm that completed the liner in 1969.

The quantities seem endless, yet, like in any great hotel, a constant effort must be made to renew or replace anything beginning to show signs of aging or wear. The reputation for excellence of a great five-star hotel is not easy to gain and requires attention to detail in order to retain it.

CHAPTER FIVE

Trafalgar House, Cunard,
and the Queen Elizabeth 2

The summer of 1971 saw a fundamental change in the ownership of the Cunard Steam-Ship Company Limited. After an independent existence of 131 years Cunard was the object of a successful take-over bid by the British company Trafalgar House Investments, Ltd. For some weeks Cunard shares had been rising on the London Stock Exchange, a clear indication of a take-over bid when a company has not announced any great profits or new endeavors to warrant optimism. News articles involved a number of potential suitors during the month of June, and Cunard was forced to acknowledge that negotiations were underway with an undisclosed party.

Trafalgar House was interested in the Cunard Line because it complemented their hotel and leisure interests. The aquisition also offered substantial tax advantages. Trafalgar House had a 10% holding in Cunard, which was then the maximum allowed before public disclosure of interest was required. They also knew that another company, Slater, Walker Securities held 11.6%, so they arranged for brokers to obtain them on their behalf. On June 30, 1971, Nigel Broackes, the chairman of Trafalgar House, informed Sir Basil Smallpeice that they now had a holding of over 21% in Cunard and that they were going to make a bid for the shipping line.

The initial £24 million offer made by Trafalgar was met with resistance by Cunard and some of the shareholders. When the value of the company was

The QUEEN ELIZABETH 2 glides through the calm waters of the majestic Geiranger Fjord in Norway on her celebrated North Cape cruise.

increased to £27.3 million, Cunard agreed to the take-over. In a message to Cunard Line employees the chairman stated that the Trafalgar House bid was accepted. "Cunard Line have now received all the assurances they requested from Trafalgar about Cunard's future role in the British shipping industry." In addition, the chairman noted, "Trafalgar House have given assurances that if their bid is successful Cunard will remain as a shipping company within the Trafalgar Group and will continue as a major force in the British shipping industry, also that QE2 will continue to operate under the British flag." Sir Basil Smallpeice asked "all Cunard staff afloat and ashore to continue unabated their efforts to ensure the company's future prosperity and their own place within it wherever the future ownership of the company's shares may lie."

On August 26, 1971, Victor Matthews of Trafalgar House Investments Ltd., took over as the chairman of the Cunard Steam-Ship Company Ltd.

The QUEEN ELIZABETH 2 was acknowledged by the new owners as a potential money maker, and the orders Cunard had placed for new tonnage were praised. But some of the existing assets of the company did not appear so financially attractive, notably, the CARMANIA and FRANCONIA, both of which Cunard had been trying to sell. The new management of Cunard announced the withdrawal from service of the two ships in October 1971 and their subsequent lay-up awaiting sale.

During the summer season of 1971 the QUEEN ELIZABETH 2 continued to hold her reputation for carrying the rich and the famous across the Atlantic. Julie Andrews and Leslie Caron crossed in July. The holds of the QUEEN accommodate automobiles and are frequently occupied by vintage machines, stately limousines, and racing cars. Robin Ormes, the motor racing ace, shipped his Lola car to participate in the Watkins Glen Six Hour International Sports Car Race on July 24, 1971. The Lola previously had been owned by Roger Penske, who had won the 1969 Daytona 24 Hour Race.

The maiden arrival of the QUEEN ELIZABETH 2 in Boston caused quite a stir. The QUEEN stopped en route from New York to Le Havre on October 1, 1971, to embark 300 members of the Honorable Artillery Company of Massachusetts. That organization was the first military company chartered in the Western hemisphere when it was created in 1638, and has been in existence ever since. In 1971 they decided to cross the ocean on the QUEEN ELIZABETH 2 to have their 334th Field Day Tour of Duty in England. The huge liner was suitably dressed for the occasion, with all flags flying, as an armada of small craft greeted her. Cunard's association with the port of Boston goes back to the very inception of the transatlantic service in 1840. There has always been a warm and close regard between the people of New England and the line. Everything went off without a hitch in spite of a dock strike, although Cunard shore personnel had to help with the loading of the luggage. The official welcoming ceremonies included the presentation of a Cunard flag to the city of Boston. The Ancient Honorable Artillery Company in full dress

The transportation of passengers' cars can be a major drawing card for the QUEEN, since she can accommodate around forty vehicles. Depending upon the facilities available and the nature of the tide, cars can be driven on through one of the nine shell doors in the sides of the ship, or lifted on by derrick and lowered through the hatch.

A major transformation of the external appearance of the QUEEN occurred in 1972 with the addition of ten penthouse suites on the sports deck slightly behind the mast. The preliminary work was done while the liner was at sea during the summer of 1972 and the prefabricated suites were lifted on board at Southampton during the annual refit at Vosper Thornycroft in the fall.

The addition of the penthouse suites gave the QE2 additional superlative accommodations, which are very popular. The preparations on the ship and the prefabrication of the units at Vosper Thornycroft had to be to a very high level of exactness for the pieces to fit.

marched from Fanueil Hall, the upper floor of which has been the AHAC armory since 1746, to Commonwealth Pier, where they were welcomed on board the QUEEN. Cunard had made arrangements for a flag of the Honorable Artillery Company to be broken out at the mast head upon their reception.

R. B. Patton, president of Cunard (North America), fitted his comments to the jocular nature of the occasion when he said:

> I also want to thank the Commodore for his hospitality this morning. At this hour, the British often enjoy a different sort of beverage, but ever since another party on board a British ship got a little out of hand, we've made it a rule to put the tea under guard while in Boston Harbor. But this is truly an occasion that calls for champagne—to describe it in appropriate terms, the greatest ship in the world has come to the hub of the universe.

Patton concluded: "To the Ancient and Honorable Artillery Company, welcome aboard and *bon voyage*; you honor us by choosing our ship. We're proud and happy to have such a distinguished send off on our first sailing."

When the QUEEN docked at Southampton on October 6, the AHAC was met by a Royal Marine band and Regimental Colonel Brian Davis of the Honourable Artillery Company of London, the oldest British regiment. In the seventeenth century some of the HAC members had emigrated to New England and provided the nucleus of the Ancient Honorable Artillery Company. The highlight of the visit of the AHAC to the mother country was a meeting with Her Majesty Queen Elizabeth II and Prince Philip at Buckingham Palace, where a silver tea set was presented to the Queen and a silver plate to the Duke of Edinburgh.

In the first six months of their ownership, Trafalgar House undertook a complete survey of the QUEEN ELIZABETH 2 and the services she could provide. It was decided that £1 million would be spent on improvements to the ship. These included modifications to the restaurants and the construction and installation of the luxury penthouse suites on Signal and Sports decks.

The 1972 season on the North Atlantic was enlivened by some violent storms and the presence of an enormous amount of ice in the steamer lanes. Captain Mortimer Hehir commanded the QUEEN on a memorable crossing April 16–23, 1972, when a violent storm raged across the North Atlantic for 1,500 miles with 50-foot seas and 100-mph winds. The horrendous conditions continued for four days. At times when one looked around there was nothing to be seen but spume and spray in all directions. On arrival at Southampton, certificates were passed out to the 1,000 passengers who had "survived" the worst storm in memory, champagne was made available to all, and flowers were offered to the ladies.

Certainly one of the most bizarre crossings the QUEEN ELIZABETH 2 ever experienced began when the liner sailed from New York shortly after 2000 hours on Monday, May 15, 1972. The QUEEN was carrying 421 first, 1,108 tourist, and 907 crew members, with Captain William J. Law in command. In mid-Atlantic on Wednesday evening the captain received a coded message from Charles Dickson of the New York office of the Cunard Line that there was a bomb threat on board the liner. The threat had been made known to Cunard in New York and it was confirmed from London that there might be two accomplices traveling on the ship. Captain Law initiated every possible security arrangement in cooperation with his senior officers, and a discreet search was carried out, but nothing was found.

The ministry of defense in London was alerted and plans coordinated to enable bomb disposal experts to board the QE2 in mid-Atlantic. Captain Law made the following announcement over the public address system to passengers at 1600 hours on Thursday:

> Ladies and Gentlemen, we have received information concerning a threat of a bomb explosion on board this ship some time during this voyage. We have received such threats in the past which have so far always turned out to be hoaxes. However, we always take them seriously and take every possible precaution.
>
> On this occasion we are being assisted by the British government, who are sending out bomb disposal experts who will be parachuted into the sea and picked up by boat and brought on board. I will, of course, keep you fully informed about the situation. Cunard are taking every precaution ashore and on board and will take any necessary action to minimize risk. If

Comparisons of the QUEEN ELIZABETH 2 with other vessels are difficult to envision, but in this scene of the old and the new, the Portuguese tall ship SAGRES is shown passing the QUEEN.

there is any question of it being necessary to pay over money, this will be done ashore in New York.

I can only ask you to remain calm. On these occasions lots of rumors tend to circulate. Please only take notice of any information that comes from me direct or from one of my officers. That is all for the moment.

At 1636 hours the QUEEN began to reduce speed prior to rendezvousing with an RAF "Nimrod" (jet reconnaissance aircraft) from St. Mawgan's in Cornwell in a position 740 miles due east of Cape Race, Newfoundland. The Nimrod was in sight at 1706 hours, positioning was verified, communication assured, and the QE2 slowed to a stop at 1734 hours in a position 45.8 degrees North and 35.1 degrees West. A little less than half an hour later, at 1808 hours an RAF Hercules was sighted carrying the four members of the bomb disposal team. Crews for two of the QE2's launches were standing by when the Hercules was sighted, and one was immediately lowered, with First Officer Robin Woodall in charge. As the QE2 and the launch headed into the wind, the pilot of the Hercules made a few preliminary runs to decide on the best approach. The height of cloud base was only 400 feet above sea level, which was too low for a safe parachute jump to be made. It was therefore necessary for the pilot to bring his plane in below the cloud level, sight the launch, and then climb quickly up through the clouds to about 800 feet. A few seconds later, although it seemed like an eternity, the first two parachutes drifted down out of the clouds. Two such runs were made, releasing two parachutists at a time, and dropping them with great precision near the QE2's launch. The QUEEN's experienced boat crew had all four parachutists in the launch within five minutes of their landing. The bomb disposal experts wore frogman suits and carried a considerable amount of equipment and, as a special consideration, a London newspaper for the Captain. Most of the QUEEN ELIZABETH 2's passengers were on deck to view the splashdowns and cheered the successful proceedings. It would have been difficult not to have been thrilled by the operation and the courage of the individuals concerned. The Hercules turned back eastward to her base in England some 1,380 miles away, but the Nimrod stayed around until the QE2's launch was safely aboard the liner. She then bade the QUEEN farewell and returned to Cornwall. The QUEEN ELIZABETH 2 was underway again at 1924 hours.

As the entertainment for the evening commenced, the bomb disposal experts began a systematic search of the ship from stem to stern. Those courageous gentlemen were Captain Robert Williams (29) and Sergeant Clifford Oliver (32) of the Royal Ordnance Corps and Lieutenant Richard Clifford (26) and Corporal Thomas Jones (28) of the Royal Marine amphibious training unit at Poole. No explosive devices of any nature were ever discovered and the QE2 safely arrived at Cherbourg and Southampton with her passengers and crew.

The departure of the QE2 from Corner Brook, Newfoundland, in August 1983 on one of her Canadian cruises sees Captain Robert Arnott and others out on the wing of the bridge keeping a hawk eye on the progress being made as the two bow thrusters, working in combination with the twin propellers, ease the QUEEN away from an unfamiliar berth.

In New York the scene had been one of considerable tension for Charles Dickson, Cunard's vice-president, who had received the anonymous telephone call about the supposed bombs and ransom demand. The caller appeared to know what he was talking about and commented that, while the gang had considered asking for $1 million, they had settled on a ransom of $350,000 in exchange for not blowing up the ship. The caller refused to say when he would call back, so the Cunard office telephones were manned day and night. In London the chairman of Cunard Line, Victor Matthews, was alerted in the middle of the night and agreed to the ransom payment, which was assembled in New York and placed in a briefcase for delivery when so ordered. Charles Dickson was given a runaround by the anonymous caller, but no one ever appeared to collect the money.

The American police and the Federal Bureau of Investigation worked day and night on the case, although remaining in the background until the QE2 safely reached Europe. Ultimately a man from New York was arrested and charged with extortion. He was tried in the Manhattan Federal Court, found guilty, and given the maximum possible sentence of 20 years. Sentencing him, the judge said: "Your actions were reprehensible and unforgivable. You took deliberate advantage of a reign of terror for very substantial gain."

An unfortunate result of the bomb threat with all its ramifications was that Cunard decided no longer to permit unrestricted access to the liner for the general public or for individuals seeing passengers off. Accordingly, the long-standing tradition of the on board Bon Voyage Party was canceled, and future passengers have had to bid their fond farewells on the pier.

During the spring of 1972 reports were received from the U.S. and Canadian meterological offices that there was a large area of ice south of Newfoundland. The ice, drifting from the Labrador Basin, had not traveled so far south for over thirty years. Because of the warnings, the QE2 had to take a course 100 miles to the south of her usual route.

On passage from Cherbourg to New York during the small hours of August 21, 1972, the QUEEN ELIZABETH 2 reduced speed to rendezvous with the U.S. Coast Guard cutter HAMILTON, which was being used as an ocean weather-observing station known as DELTA. One of her seamen, W. D. Emmett, received word that a member of his family was critically ill, and an inquiry had been made if there was any possibility of assistance from the QUEEN ELIZABETH 2. On this occasion a launch was sent over from the other ship, and within eight minutes of her being alongside the QE2 had ordered full speed ahead for her destination.

Prosperity in the shipping division was reflected in Trafalgar House's announced plans to build another cruise liner. During the naming ceremony of the CUNARD AMBASSADOR at Rotterdam on October 21, 1972, Victor Matthews said the hull and engines of the new liner will be built by Burmeister Wein of Copenhagen and the fitting out will be accomplished in Italy by INMA

The Gare Maritime at Cherbourg plays host to the QUEEN ELIZABETH 2 on a number of occasions each year. Originally built to accommodate the QUEEN MARY and QUEEN ELIZABETH, the French terminal is the only remaining one the QE2 uses regularly that served the older QUEENS. The giant passageways descend to meet the appropriate doors on the side of the liner.

Entering New York at the end of an Atlantic run, the bow of the QUEEN ELIZABETH 2 is highlighted by the early morning sun. She has just cleared the Verrazano Narrows Bridge, and seasoned travelers may just be stirring from their beds while those who have not experienced an arrival by sea in New York Harbor will have been up for some time to see the sights.

of La Spezia (three British yards had declined to tender for the contract). The order for a sister ship was placed in January 1973. The two ships entered service as the CUNARD COUNTESS and the CUNARD PRINCESS.

In 1973 the QUEEN offered two "Silver Anniversary Cruises to Israel" under the auspices of Assured Travel Services, Inc., of Massachusetts designed to cover the Passover/Easter (April 14–28, 1973) holiday and the twenty-fifth anniversary celebrations for Israel (April 28–May 13, 1973). They attracted a considerable amount of publicity and it was feared by many that the ship was vunerable to an attack by Arab terrorists. As a result of these fears, and in consultation with the British ministry of defense, very strict security measures were taken throughout the cruise.

When the QE2 arrived at Southampton from her Caribbean cruise on April 12, 1973, the Southampton Ocean Terminal was sealed off from the public and armed guards went aboard. Meanwhile Royal Navy skin divers kept vigil over the underwater hull of the QUEEN as she took on stores and awaited her passengers.

The QUEEN sailed from Southampton with only about 600 passengers, less than a third of her capacity, and returned from Israel on the second cruise with approximately the same number. Certainly adverse publicity and heightened security concern took its toll on the bookings. For those who did make the cruise to Israel, or back, there was a fabulous opportunity to enjoy the ship and be pampered with a crew–passenger ratio of two to one.

Special arrangements were made to provide a complete kosher service for the large percentage of Jewish passengers. The entire Columbia kitchen and restaurant were made kosher for the cruise, conforming with the highest standards of kashruth.

First stop on the cruise itinerary of the QUEEN ELIZABETH 2 was a call at Lisbon, Portugal, April 17, 1973. Portuguese authorities were very concerned about security and even went so far as to halt all traffic on the giant suspension bridge spanning the Tagus River while the QUEEN passed beneath the soaring span. The Lisbon passenger terminal was closed to all visitors, and passengers were searched before being permitted to rejoin the ship if they went ashore. After leaving Lisbon, the QUEEN set course for Israel. The ship was under orders to complete the final day's voyage to Israel at her maximum speed and to extinguish all unnecessary external lights. Her arrival on April 21 marked the inaugural visit of the QE2 to Israel and a unique occasion for the town of Ashdod—the first visit ever of a passenger liner to the port. Ashdod is a convenient departure point for land tours to Jerusalem, only 44 miles away, and other points of interest. The liner stayed four days at Ashdod and then proceeded to Haifa for a similar period.

On April 29 the passengers from the Easter/Passover Cruise flew home and the passengers for the Silver Independence Day Cruise joined the ship for a reversal of the itinerary until the QE2 sailed from Ashdod on May 8 for the return voyage to Southampton via Palma de Mallorca. The liner returned safely to Britain on May 13, 1973.

Over a year later, on July 16, 1974, President Anwar Sadat of Egypt revealed in a BBC television interview with Lord Chalfont, former minister of state at the Foreign and Commonwealth Office, that he personally had countermanded an order given to an Egyptian submarine commander by an Arab leader to torpedo the QUEEN ELIZABETH 2 during her cruise to Israel. Subsequently a debate ensued as to whether or not the submarine, an ex-Russia Romeo type, had the capability to catch the 28.5-knot QE2. It was generally regarded that the submarine, with a maximum surface speed of 19 knots, could not have intercepted the liner.

The future for the QUEEN ELIZABETH 2 certainly brightened with the announcement that the liner would sail on her first world cruise on January 4, 1975, a 91-day odyssey through the Panama Canal and around the world. The total cruise beginning and ending in Southampton would cover 37,963 miles and take the QUEEN on an easterly course to more than twenty major ports around the globe. Norman Thompson, Cunard's managing director at the time, told the press, "We think QE2 is the best ship afloat for this type of cruise"—a remark subsequently acknowledged by the fact that a long cruise has been made annually ever since.

A major event on any world cruise always is the arrival in Hong King. The point of origin for many land tours to the People's Republic of China, the Crown Colony of Hong Kong also is a picturesque tourist center and a fabulous marketplace all of its own.

The QE2 returned to the North Atlantic for the 1973 season with high hopes for her most successful season ever. Americans were preparing to travel more as the recession lessened and business conditions improved.

An unusual voyage made by the QUEEN ELIZABETH 2 was in the summer of 1973, when the ship was chartered for a cruise to Come by Chance, Newfoundland, in honor of the opening of the new oil refinery on the shores of Placentia Bay. The liner docked at the pier of the Newfoundland Refining Company, which soon would be hosting supertankers transporting the products from the 100,000-barrel a day refinery. John M. Shaheen, chairman of NRC, said: "Chartering the QE2 allowed us to give everybody a first hand look at the year round, deep water, docking facilities available in Placentia Bay, which is one of the major reasons for locating the refinery at Come By Chance." The invited guests aboard the QUEEN included representatives from major oil, financial, shipping, engineering, and construction interests.

The winter 1973 season brought a three-day cruise from New York to chase the comet Kohoutek, expected to be one of the brightest comets of the twentieth century. The cruise was completely sold out when the QUEEN sailed from New York on December 9 on the "comet watch." Guest of honor on board the liner was the Czech-born astronomer Professor Lubos Kohoutek, who first identified the comet in March 1973 and predicted its brilliance. Dr. Isaac Asimov, the famous scientist and science fiction writer, was also booked as part of the enrichment program for the cruise. Unfortunately, in this instance the weather did not provide much respite from overcast conditions and rain, which made chasing the comet futile, but later Caribbean cruises were blessed with clear air and balmy weather, which permitted passengers to easily see the comet.

Trafalgar House was determined to make the QUEEN ELIZABETH 2 pay in every way possible. In 1974 the company introduced free transatlantic airline tickets for passengers booking one way in the more expensive suites and cabins on the ship. In all, twenty-one transatlantic crossings were planned for 1974, and the schedule, whenever possible, was integrated with that of the FRANCE, since there was no point in having the two great Atlantic liners on the same side of the ocean at once.

The biggest headache Cunard Line faced in the mid-1970s was the enormous increase in the cost of bunkering oil, which went up from $20 to $70 a ton. Some critics complained that the QUEEN represented a poor use of a scarce resource. In a letter to the *London Times*, this argument was met forcefully by Norman S. Thompson, managing director, Cunard, who notes that the fuel consumption of the QE2 over a 3,060-mile transatlantic voyage at a speed of 28½ knots was approximately 1.55 tons per individual when she was carrying 1,500 passengers, which was relatively efficient in comparison with comparable vessels.

One activity that could generate good publicity and profit for the QE2 was

The towering side of the QUEEN ELIZ-ABETH 2 stretches to the heavens in the view of passengers departing from the QUEEN by launch.

The launches of the QE2 do yeoman's duty carrying passengers back and forth from the ship in ports where she cannot berth. Designated units also serve as rescue vessels when called upon, while all, collectively, ensure the safety of the QUEEN's passengers and crew.

America's only major contribution to the superstructure of the QUEEN ELIZABETH 2 was made in 1977 when the Queen Mary and Queen Elizabeth suites were fitted forward of the 1972 penthouses during an annual refit at the Bethlehem Steel Shipyard, Bayonne, New Jersey.

a "short-term" charter. When the Election Campaign Committee for New York mayor Abraham Beame was casting around for a means of reducing the debt for the mayoralty campaign, they decided to hold a birthday party for His Honor on the QUEEN on the evening of March 21, 1974. Tickets for the novel "cruise" sold at $250 a head to 1,000 of the mayor and Mrs. Beame's closest friends. To make the whole thing more realistic, guests were given regular cruise tickets and "embarked" as though they were about to sail. Thus the ship became the scene of a very lively party and a spectacular salute to one of New York City's famous leaders.

The QUEEN ELIZABETH 2 appeared to be sailing toward a £2,000,000 profit for the 1973–1974 fiscal year when she encountered misfortune. The QUEEN was steaming some 200 miles off Bermuda around 0400 hours on April 1, 1974, when the alarm on an electronic probe designed to detect the presence of oil or other contaminants in the absolutely pure water of her boilers failed. The boilers consist of an arrangement of hundreds of pipes through which the water passes. A film of oil spread through some of these, and the furnace, instead of heating the water inside the tubes, heated the tubes themselves and damaged them. As a result, the propulsion system was shut down immediately before any further damage occurred. The ships engineers worked hard to rectify the fault, but, because this might not be done in a reasonable time, Cunard decided to leave nothing to chance and began making contingency plans. The president of Flagship Cruises in Oslo, Norway, was contacted, and arrangements were made for the M.S. SEA VENTURE, which was on a three-day visit to Bermuda, to render assistance.

Captain Torbjorn Hauge, master of the SEA VENTURE, sailed his ship almost immediately for the QE2's last position, leaving nearly 400 of his own cruise passengers ashore. Two hundred and two passengers elected to stay with the officer and crew of the SEA VENTURE to experience the adventure and assist if possible. The Bermuda authorities provided hotel accommodations for the other Flagship Cruises passengers left behind until the SEA VENTURE returned. Meanwhile Cunard chartered aircraft to meet the QE2's passengers in Bermuda and to fly them back to the United States.

At sea the QE2's passengers danced all night under the stars and regarded the whole experience as an adventure. Throughout their stay on board, they were kept fully informed at regular intervals by the master, Captain Peter Jackson, over the public address system operated from the bridge. By doing this, the master undoubtedly contributed much to the well-being and peace of mind of the passengers and relieved them of any anxiety.

The SEA VENTURE reached the QUEEN at 0330 hours on April 3, 1974, and the plans for the transfer of the QE2's passengers using the Norwegian ship's launches were formalized. The SEA VENTURE maneuvered as close as possible to the QUEEN and a calm stretch of water lay between for the transfer of the 1,654 passengers.

A thousand life jackets and twenty inflatable rubber rafts were sent over to the SEA VENTURE, because with all the passengers from the QE2 the Norwegian liner would be way over her normal complement. Disembarkation took place from two gangways on Five Deck. The first launch departed with passengers at 0805 hours, and by 1539 hours they had all left the ship. The discharge of baggage followed, and by 1745 hours the whole operation was concluded and the SEA VENTURE set her course for Hamilton.

The crew of the SEA VENTURE found accommodations for 700 in cabins, and the remainder were provided with blankets and deck chairs or portable beds in the public rooms.

An all-night buffet and free bar service were provided on the SEA VENTURE throughout the overnight trip. Additional doctors and nurses sailed with the SEA VENTURE, but their services, happily, were not needed. Most of the passengers who were taken off the QE2 gave her officers and crew high marks and were delighted with the services and total refund of their fares made by Cunard. The incident certainly ranks as one of the most difficult experiences the QUEEN has ever faced, but the prompt, efficient manner in which all aspects of the problem were handled rebounded very substantially in the goodwill of the line. Most passengers said that they hoped to travel again with Cunard in the near future.

Preliminary repairs were carried out at Bermuda, and then the QE2 returned to New York, where they were completed.

Captain Peter Jackson and the officers and crew of the QUEEN ELIZABETH 2 received a special radiogram from Victor Matthews, managing director of the Cunard Line:

THE FOLLOWING MOTION HAS BEEN TABLED IN THE HOUSE OF COMMONS TODAY BY MR. ROBERT TAYLOR CONSERVATIVE MEMBER OF PARLIAMENT FOR NORTH WEST CROYDON WHICH SPEAKS FOR ITSELF: THAT THIS HOUSE

The island of Tristan de Cunha issued one of the largest stamps in the world to honor the arrival of the QUEEN ELIZABETH 2 in one of the stops on a world cruise. Native vessels and the symbol of the Cunard Line, a gold lion rampant against a crimson background encircled by a golden rope, complete the design of the stamp.

CONGRATULATES THE MANAGEMENT OF CUNARD FOR THE EXEMPLARY MANNER IN WHICH IT DISCHARGED EVERY POSSIBLE LEGAL AND MORAL OBLIGATION TO THE PASSENGERS OF THE QE2 DURING THE RECENT VOYAGE AND CONSIDERS THAT IN SO DOING IT HAS MAINTAINED THE HIGHEST REPUTATION OF BRITISH COMMERCE.

Matthews commented that it was understood to be quite rare for a commercial organization to be so recognized in the House. He stated: "As your Chairman I would like to thank each and everyone of you who played a part in bringing this about. The strength of a team can only be judged in adverse conditions and I would particularly like to congratulate the Captain, officers and crew for their magnificent performance."

The QUEEN sailed on schedule from New York Tuesday, April 16, 1974 on her first transatlantic crossing for the season. On the way across Cunard and Dunhill sponsored the world's first backgammon tournament played aboard a liner. Players included Earl Lichfield, Liberal MP Clement Freud, and comedian Spike Milligan. The tournament was won by Charles Benson, who collected £10,000 in prize money.

On April 25, 1974, QE2 sailed on a twelve-day cruise with 1,540 passengers to the Mediterranean. When she departed, she was given a farewell salute by the British army helicopter display team, the Blue Eagles.

At Cannes a rare event occurred when the QUEEN ELIZABETH 2 and the FRANCE anchored near each other for a day and onlookers from shore could

Summer storm clouds gather over Southampton, England, just before the departure of the QUEEN ELIZABETH 2 in 1972 from the old Ocean Terminal. The starboard wing of the bridge with the bow thruster controls can be seen.

observe the two largest liners in the world. It had already been announced by the French government that the giant FRANCE was to be withdrawn at the end of the 1974 season as an economy measure, since the liner's deficit of $12 million a year had ballooned with the inflation in fuel prices. Accordingly, Cunard announced that the QE2 would increase the number of North Atlantic crossings to thirty-one for the 1975 season in a partial attempt to fill the gap and to benefit from being the only remaining transatlantic superliner.

Occasionally a New York Harbor pilot may get a longer ride than he bargained for when he takes a vessel to sea. Normally the pilot is dropped near the Ambrose Light, but on August 25, 1974, Captain John Cahill found himself a guest of the Cunard Line for an Atlantic crossing when the pilot cutter was engaged in a rescue mission and could not take him off. Accordingly, he had a five-day ocean crossing to Southampton and a free trip back by air with all the trimmings; steamship lines traditionally treat their pilots very well indeed.

Later, on September 25, 1974, while on passage from Naples to Barcelona, the eternal watchfulness of the Cunard officers on the bridge paid off handsomely for some distressed seafarers. The QUEEN ELIZABETH 2 was steaming through gale-force winds and a rough Mediterranean Sea when at 0215 hours red distress flares were sighted to the north. The QUEEN immediately answered so peremptory a summons of the sea and altered course through the heavy seas and the darkness to investigate. Fifteen minutes later, at 0230 hours, a small yacht in severe difficulty was sighted. The individuals on the yacht were incapable of doing anything, so the 963-foot QE2 had to maneuver on her two engines under the gale conditions. Six male survivors of the yacht STEPHANIE of Toulon were rescued by 0345 hours, and the QUEEN resumed passage to Barcelona. The fickleness of the sea takes some and leaves others to be rescued by a vessel beyond their wildest dreams.

When the QUEEN sailed from Southampton on January 4, 1975, she set out on her most historic voyage, 38,564 miles over 92 days to 24 ports in 19 countries across 4 continents. One of the selling points of the trip was the possibility for up to 600 passengers to have a three-day side trip to the People's Republic of China. The QUEEN left England with 342 World Cruise passengers, picked up another 570 in New York, and additional passengers in Port Everglades, Florida. Other passengers joined and left the ship at various ports around the world. By the time she returned to England, over 3,965 people had been on board at some stage of the cruise. For the last leg of the cruise between Los Angeles and New York, Cunard had a waiting list of over 300 passengers who wished to sail. Everywhere she went, the QUEEN was given a royal reception, from Cape Town to Singapore, Hong Kong to Kobe, Honolulu to Acapulco. There was rarely a dull moment. When the QUEEN passed through the Panama Canal, she became the largest ship in the world to

The maiden arrival of the QE2 at Philadelphia in honor of the 300th anniversary of the City of Brotherly Love, occurred on April 25, 1982. The liner came at the invitation of the Tercentenary Committee. A commemorative hand-cut slate by lettercutter Richard D. Grasby, visiting professor at the University of Pennsylvania, from Dorset, England, was presented by the sculptor and Dr. and Mrs. T. Noble Jarrel of Dover, Delaware, to the QUEEN ELIZABETH 2. This plaque and reception table now grace the Captain's cabin on the QUEEN.

make the transit, surpassing the German liner BREMEN (51,731 tons) in 1936. On her return to Southampton, she was greeted by the band of the Queen's Own Hussars at the Southampton Ocean Terminal and a visit from the Lord Mayor of Southampton to welcome her home.

The QUEEN's North Atlantic season proved relatively uneventful until June 20, 1975, when on passage from Cherbourg to New York she received a call at 2204 hours from the Russian trawler LUGA (2,690 tons) asking for assistance for a sick seaman, Aleck Sungayala (27) of Latvia, who was ill with a suspected burst ulcer. The QE2 altered course some 128 miles to make rendezvous with the factory ship, which was sighted at 0210 hours. By 0258 hours the sick seaman was on board the QUEEN, and four minutes later she resumed her voyage to New York.

Further away, in the Caribbean, Mrs. Neil Armstrong, wife of the astronaut, was making maritime history when she became the first American woman to christen a Cunard Line passenger vessel. Following the ceremony at San Juan on August 8, 1976, the CUNARD COUNTESS put to sea on the first of many weekly Caribbean cruises.

On March 1, 1977, the company sold the CUNARD ADVENTURE to a Norwegian company, and she was re-registered as the SOUTHWARD II. Soon after, on March 30, Her Serene Highness Princess Grace of Monaco christened Cunard Line's latest cruise liner, the CUNARD PRINCESS, at a ceremony held in New York.

The schedule for 1977 involved the Jubilee World Cruise of ninety-two days, and a series of European and Caribbean cruises in the spring and fall interspliced with thirty Atlantic crossings. In London, Trafalgar House had bought the venerable Ritz Hotel and completely refurbished it to bring the great hotel institution up to the standards of excellence for which its founder had been famous. The La Toc Hotel in St. Lucia and the Paradise Beach Hotel in Barbados continued to prove to be outstanding values in that region, with very high ratings from critics evaluating the opportunities for vacations in the Caribbean.

The June 27, 1977, sailing from Southampton coincided with the dress rehearsal for the Jubilee Review of the Fleet by Her Majesty the Queen. Passengers and crew on the QUEEN ELIZABETH 2 made the most of it by packing the rails as the cruise staff, aided by Royal Navy briefings, provided a detailed running commentary of the naval vessels as the QE2 steamed past. The loudspeakers on the QUEEN played "Land of Hope and Glory" and "Rule Britannia." There were 180 in the review line and hundreds of pleasure craft all over the water. Two Royal Navy vessels H.M.S. ARK ROYAL and H.M.S. HURON at the end of the line had to be nudged apart to allow the QUEEN through a 700-feet gap between them. The QUEEN ELIZABETH 2 exchanged salutes with vessels all the way down the line in a most majestic departure from Southampton.

Her Serene Highness Princess Grace of Monaco christens the new cruise ship CUNARD PRINCESS during a visit to New York, March 30, 1977. Earlier Mrs. Neil Armstrong, wife of the first man on the moon, christened the sister ship CUNARD COUNTESS at San Juan, Puerto Rico, August 8, 1976.

For economic reasons, it was decided that the 1977 annual refit would be carried out by the Bethlehem Steel Corporation of Bayonne, New Jersey. By having the refit in the United States, the ship was able to start the winter cruise season earlier, without having to make late winter crossings of the North Atlantic at a time of the year when they are not very well subscribed. Work included the renewal of one of the turbines. The turbine, weighing 17 tons, had to be flown out in a Lockhead Hercules aircraft from the makers, John Brown Engineering of Scotland. The dock yard also constructed and fitted the most luxurious rooms on the ship, known as the Queen Elizabeth and Queen Mary Suites.

One more rescue can be listed to the credit of the QUEEN ELIZABETH 2—during the hours of daylight, for a change. On passage from Cherbourg to New York, August 16, 1977, a message was received at 1000 hours from the French trawler DRAKKER of Dieppe saying that they required assistance for an injured seaman. The QUEEN altered course and rendezvoused with the DRAKKER. A launch was sent away from QE2 to collect the seaman, who was safely on board by 1120 hours. The French seaman, Claude Leleu, was admitted to the ship's hospital and treated for leg injuries, from which he fully recovered.

The desire to produce variety in the QUEEN's schedule resulted in a Great Pacific and Oriental Cruise in 1978. The history-making 39,057-mile cruise saw visits to Australia, New Zealand, and the Philippines, during which the QUEEN ELIZABETH 2 visited thirty-one ports, twelve that she had never been to before.

Captain T. D. Ridley, R.D., R.N.R., was in command when the QUEEN ELIZABETH 2 experienced one of the worst storms of her career during a North Atlantic crossing in September 1978. The liner encountered a storm front laying across the shipping lanes which gave little choice for maneuvering.

The QUEEN ELIZABETH 2 steams along after her American refit in 1977, with the new Queen Mary and Queen Elizabeth suites in place immediately aft the forward mast. The penthouses are clearly visible in this aerial shot.

The winds built up to force 12 (the maximum on the Beaufort scale) and the waves were 50 feet high, which is to say over 100 feet from trough to crest. Captain Ridley commented that it was one of the three worst storms he had experienced in thirty-five years at sea. At one point a wall of water hit the liner broadside on the bow and crumpled the iron railing, while on other occasions colossal waves reached as high as the bridge. According to a *Newsweek* article of September 25, 1978, a lady had asked Captain Ridley if he had considered asking the coast guard for assistance during the worst of the storm. Ridley had replied: "Madame, first there was no need for help. And, secondly, if there had been a Coast Guard cutter in the area, the QUEEN would have had to help the *Coast Guard*."

The QUEEN ELIZABETH 2 reached her tenth birthday in 1979, and the 1979–1980 period was celebrated appropriately as a milestone in her career. The 1979 world cruise, with the theme "For once in your life, live!" went to twenty-four ports in fourteen countries. Especially historical was the inaugural call at Darien, the first time in recent history a passenger liner from the Western world ever docked in the People's Republic of China. During the call, the Joe Loss band played at a concert attended by more than 1,700 Chinese, again the first show band ever to do so. Another inaugural visit was that to the Island of Tristian da Cunha in the South Atlantic. In honor of the ship's arrival, they produced the longest British Commonwealth stamp ever issued!.

During her tenth anniversary year the QUEEN also was the subject of a National Geographic film about the great ocean liners. The film had enormous coverage in the United States and was shown by popular demand several times on American television. Entitled "The End of an Era," it resulted in a new awareness about a vanishing piece of maritime heritage and the fact that the QUEEN ELIZABETH 2 was the last great transatlantic liner. During her first decade in service the QUEEN had steamed a phenomenal 1½ million miles and carried the British flag to sixty-three nations around the world.

The QUEEN has more than her share of heroes. On October, 24, 1979, she was in harbor at Las Palmas when an elderly passenger fell into the harbor. Four QE2 crew members who saw the accident did not hesitate to jump to the rescue. They were cruise director Brian Price, cruise staff Eric Mason and George Schofiled, and deputy chief engineer Stanley Child. The four men dived between the ship and quayside in very deep water and, although they dragged the passenger to shore, he died approximately a month later without leaving the hospital. Captain Douglas Ridley congratulated the men on their courage, and Bernard Crisp, Cunard's marketing director, presented them with awards. Crisp said: "Some of us go through life never having the opportunity to find out if we are really brave. I believe anybody on this ship would have done what you did—but the difference is that you actually did it."

The 1979 refit was also undertaken by Bethlehem Steel Corporation at Bayonne between November 21 and December 21, 1979, and resulted in extensive work on the boilers in cooperation with the British firm of Foster-Wheeler, Ltd., which designed and built the units originally. The complete overhaul of auxiliary equipment was undertaken, as well as work on one propeller, the stabilizers, and some bilge plating. What is most important to passengers, of course, is what they see and, perhaps, how they see it. The 1979 refit included the replacement of 25,000 fluorescent light bulbs to put a shine on the facelift, along with 20 miles of carpeting, and the repainting of her hull with self-polishing paint.

During the Tenth Anniversary World Cruise the largest number of passengers ever were carried on the ship. Individuals were able to book for portions of the cruise, thus accommodations were sufficient. One of the highlights of the trip was the maiden transit of the Suez Canal, making the QE2 the largest ship ever to transit both the Suez and Panama canals in the same voyage. The inaugural call to Yalta on the shores of the Black Sea was cut unexpectedly short. As passengers were preparing to go ashore in the

The CUNARD PRINCESS (1977) glides through the waters of Glacial Bay in Alaska during one of her summer cruises along the inland waterway to Alaska.

launches, the Russian authorities decided that every shore-going passenger must have a Soviet visa. As soon as this was brought to his attention, Captain R. H. Arnott knew right away that the process of carrying out their wishes would take so long that some of the passengers would never get ashore. Without any further ado, he ordered all the officials off the ship and put to sea again as the stirring music of "Rule Britannia" played throughout the liner.

The officers of the QUEEN were able to contribute something to the solution of an Atlantic mystery in June 1980. The two-masted schooner EL PIRATA en route from Boston to Kristiansand, Norway, had not been seen or heard from since June 11 and was reported overdue by Portishead Radio. On June 22 the schooner was sighted by the QE2 923 miles from Lands End. All was reported well, except that problems had been experienced with their radio.

The 1981 world cruise of the QUEEN ELIZABETH 2 was dubbed "The Six Continent Odyssey" and began from New York on January 18, 1981. It would take the QUEEN around the world on an eastward course through the Panama Canal and across the Pacific for a total distance of 32,946 miles in eighty days.

Upon returning from the world cruise, the QE2 sailed into a sea of labor troubles at Southampton docks. As a result of the upset, she was unable to store much in the way of provisions and had to make adjustments to take on supplies at a number of cruise ports, notably Lisbon. In May 1981 she also had to terminate a cruise at Cherbourg and to turn around there when dockers, who had refused to handle the passengers of the P & O liner CANBERRA, also

An official French Line portrait of the FRANCE (1962) shows the distinctive flukes on her funnels designed to carry the smoke and soot clear of the "longest liner in the world." The QUEEN ELIZABETH 2 was the great competitor of the FRANCE for five years until her withdrawal from service in 1974. Subsequently she was bought by Norwegian Caribbean Lines, rebuilt, and renamed the NORWAY.

refused to serve the QUEEN. The 1981 transatlantic season began from Cherbourg as the result of Southampton labor unrest. On May 22, when the ship was preparing to sail, the crane drivers would not lift off the gangway. Captain Douglas Ridley instructed his sailors to cut it off with gas torches in order to permit the liner to sail on a Norwegian cruise. A major modernization of the facilities at Southampton resulted in the closing of the old Southampton Ocean Terminal, which had served all three QUEENS and many other big ships for forty years. In its place the new Queen Elizabeth II Terminal was created for the handling of the passengers and luggage from the QUEEN and opened in April 1981.

During the summer 1981 season the QE2 called at Bar Harbor, Maine, on a Canadian cruise that proved very popular, with some 1,750 passengers on board. Cunard designated the crossing from New York to Southampton July 25–30, 1981 the "QE2 Royal Wedding Commemorative Voyage." The ship was decorated in honor of the Prince and Princess of Wales and special programs and lectures were given during the crossing. As a finale a specially made film of the royal wedding in St. Paul's Cathedral was flown out to the QUEEN by helicopter for showing in the theater during the last day out. Passengers were delighted with the experience and expressed their appreciation to Cunard for not having missed one of the events of the century.

Four television camera crews and several news reporters were on the quay to meet the ship when she arrived in New York with a stowaway from a Bahamas cruise. Piccolo, a mongrel that lives near the pier at West 49th Street, had slipped aboard the ship in search of food. He was smart enough to pick a voyage when there were no other dogs, so he enjoyed the luxury of his own blond kennel maid and a choice of quarters.

In 1982 the QUEEN ELIZABETH 2 was invited to Philadelphia for the celebrations in connection with the 300th anniversary of the city, "Century Four." The events in connection with this maiden voyage to Delaware Bay and what followed would make for one of the most exciting episodes in the life of the QUEEN.

CHAPTER SIX

The Falklands

Preparing the QUEEN ELIZABETH 2 for her duties as a troop transport—helicopter carrier included the construction of an after flight deck for helicopters on the stern of the ship. The aft flight deck would accommodate two landing pads (Two and Three, with One forward). The QE2 and all other commercial vessels requisitioned were designated STUFT (Ships Taken Up From Trade).

The maiden arrival of the QUEEN ELIZABETH 2 in Philadelphia on April 25, 1982, was all that anyone could have desired. The liner was greeted by beautiful weather over Delaware Bay from the moment she picked up the pilot at Lewes, Delaware. As she made her way upstream toward Philadelphia, she was greeted by millions of the citizens of Delaware, New Jersey, and Pennsylvania, who lined the coastline to see the QUEEN steam by. A veritable sea of humanity packed the broad container wharf at the Packer Marine Terminal just to get a glimpse of the liner as she dominated the river skyline. Some 12,000 privileged souls paid $50 to $500 each for the pleasure of either breakfast, cocktails, or dinner on the QUEEN ELIZABETH 2. This was imperative, because, insofar as Cunard was concerned, if the QUEEN was to remain at her pier in Philadelphia, then she had to earn her daily expenses through her kitchen and restaurant activities. Accordingly, charities were encouraged to arrange elaborate fund raisers through festivities on the ship. The special occasion for the QUEEN ELIZABETH 2's maiden arrival in Philadelphia was the grand opening of "Century Four," the year-long tricentennial celebration (1682–1982) of the founding of the city of Philadelphia by William Penn. The reception given the QUEEN was exuberant, even if security precautions were tight. In addition to the normal concern over Northern Ireland, the outbreak of hostilities between Great Britain and Argentina over the Falkland Islands (Malvinas) some 8,000 miles away in the wintry South Atlantic had heightened concern. The U.S. Coast Guard vessels were very much in evidence on the Delaware River. Whatever might have been going on elsewhere, summer conditions prevailed in Philadelphia and the maiden visit of the QUEEN ELIZABETH 2 was both a success commercially and an overwhelming triumph in terms of public relations. Every newspaper, radio, and television station had covered the arrival and stay of the largest passenger liner to dock in Philadelphia. Not since the old American Line had launched its ships from the William Cramp Shipyard in the latter part of the nineteenth century had there been so much excitement centered on the waterfront. Even when the QE2 departed from Philadelphia around noon on April 29, every small vantage point along her route to the sea was packed once again with people eager to see her off. As she left the narrow reaches of the Delaware River for the broader expanses of Delaware Bay, she appeared extraordinarily majestic and powerful, with a thin plume of smoke trailing from her funnel against the late afternoon sky. A brief stop at Lewes to drop the pilot near the old stone ice breakers and the QUEEN ELIZABETH 2 put out to sea for what everyone thought would be a normal run to England.

All of the QUEEN's officers were concerned about developments in the South Atlantic, but few thought there was much likelihood of the QE2 taking part in the hostilities. First Officer Philip Rentell and Second Officer Paul Lowett were on the bridge for the 8–12 watch when they became interested in calculating the fuel, time, and distance factors at various speeds for a run from England to the Falklands. These calculations were filling a note pad when Captain Alexander J. Hutcheson came up behind the two junior officers and saw what they were doing. Laughingly Hutcheson said, "You two will have us down there yet!" Within days the statistical information would be of value. The officers on the bridge calculated that the QUEEN ELIZABETH 2 would cover the 8,000-mile route at a speed of 27½ knots over 10½ days, during which her engines would gulp an awesome 6,000 tons of oil. That oil would have a retail value of £1,080,000 at $180 per ton for the one-way trip.

The news that the QUEEN ELIZABETH 2 actually was to be requisitioned for trooping duties came as something of a shock and through unofficial channels. On May 3, as the QUEEN steamed along the southern coast of England bound for Southampton, those on the Cunarder listening to the 1230 BBC news heard that their ship had been requisitioned by the government. One of the radio officers came up to the bridge with the news, but when Captain Hutcheson was phoned by an enterprising BBC reporter and asked about the requisitioning, all he could say was that he knew nothing about it officially. Needless to say, there was some feeling that the ship's officers could have been given some forewarning of these developments, but it was learned later that the news had been prematurely released in London. Following confirmation, Captain Hutcheson made a formal announcement to passengers and crew shortly after 1300 hours that the QE2 would be withdrawn from commercial service upon arrival at Southampton. The QE2 was due to dock late that evening at the Queen Elizabeth 2 Terminal and, as she steamed up the Channel with all her lights ablaze, there was considerable excitement on board. The QUEEN ELIZABETH 2 officially came alongside her berth at two minutes past midnight on May 4, 1982, and was immediately requisitioned for war service. The run from Philadelphia to Southampton was 3,203 miles and had been accomplished at an average speed of 27.19 knots. Later that morning 1,600 passengers disembarked after breakfast between 0900 and 1030 hours, and various normal cleaning-up chores were done for the remainder of the day. At 2200 hours that evening tugs carefully swung the 963-foot liner–troopship around in the turning basin so that her starboard side lay against the quay.

The conversion work began on May 5 to prepare the ship for her trooping assignment. The amazing adaptability of large modern helicopters made the broad open expanses of the QUEEN's decks both fore and aft perfectly suited for the aircraft with just a "few, minor" alterations. Chief Officer Ronald Warwick and First Officer Rentell went over the plans of the ship with Lieutenant Comander David Poole of the Royal Navy and then escorted him around the open decks. Suddenly the immensity of the task sunk in as decisions were made to slice off the upper deck Lido in line with the Q4 bar (now the "Club Lido" Bar), as well as all the associated superstructure down to the quarterdeck level. This would enable the after end of the QE2 to be

Below the new flight deck it was necessary to strengthen the structure in order to provide firm landing platforms for the helicopters and their loads.

A portion of the ammunition carried by the QUEEN was intended for troop practice sessions. Firing exercises frequently took place from the boat deck, at small floating targets released from a forward shell door as they swept by the liner. Care had to be taken to restrain enthusiasm so that no bullets came too near the liner.

Critical to the success of the QUEEN ELIZABETH 2 as a troop transport and helicopter carrier was the ability to refuel the vessel. A practice refueling exercise with R.F.A. GREY ROVER occurred along the south coast of England soon after the QUEEN began her voyage.

converted into one huge landing pad and service area for helicopters. Forward the decision was made to extend the quarterdeck toward the bow and over the capstan machinery in order to create a landing pad there. The question of what would support the enormous weight of the steel pads and the 18,626 pounds (8,449 kilograms) of a Sea King helicopter plus whatever it might be called upon to carry was critical. The two outdoor swimming pools aft were the answer; they were designed to hold tons of seawater and therefore could supply the foundation for the flight deck. Steel plates were laid over the bottoms of the pools to support and distribute the weight of a network of vertical girders.

Communications in any war situation always remain critical, and an independent radio room was especially constructed behind the bridge. Since the QUEEN could not carry fuel for much more than a one-way trip, provisions had to be made for refueling the giant liner at sea. Pipes were laid from the starboard midship's baggage entrance on Two Deck to the huge tanks of the liner six decks below. The potential peril involved in refueling the QUEEN at sea with heavy oil coursing through piping that ran through prime passenger areas and then down to the vulnerable propulsion system was considerable and caused some trepidation.

Between May 5 and May 9 most of the decorative pictures and valuable furniture were removed from the ship and stored in warehouses ashore. All plants also had to go, as well as the casino equipment—definitely not needed on this voyage, when Lady Luck would have her hands full with other matters. The QUEEN's own china, glassware, and silverware were collected, packed, and stored. In an effort to protect the carpeting, sheets of hardboard were laid over all carpets in the public rooms, passage ways, stairways, and in some of the cabins. The boards were successful only in areas experiencing light usage. During the voyage it became necessary to remove the hardboard covering in the vicinity of "D" Stairway near the entrance to the Columbia Dining Room because the boards were deteriorating under heavy use and the carpet was being destroyed. Some of the famous deep-blue carpet of the "D" Stairway was taken up and stored, exposing the bare deck, which could better withstand the beating. In other areas the carpet would have to be replaced when the QUEEN returned from trooping duties.

As the QUEEN received tons upon tons of military stores and equipment, the news was received that H.M.S. SHEFFIELD, a British destroyer, had been hit by an Exocet missile fired from an Argentinian Super Etendard plane. There were heavy casualties as a result, including twenty dead. The sinking of the SHEFFIELD followed by two days the torpedoing of the second largest ship in the Argentinian navy, the GENERAL BELGRANO (ex U.S.S. PHOENIX), which sunk in the icy waters of the South Atlantic. The war clearly was heating up for both sides with grievous losses in men and ships. Suddenly Cunard officers and crew who were being given sporadic leave began to be more concerned about writing wills and setting their personal affairs in order.

The equipment coming on the QUEEN included hundreds of extra life jackets and additional safety appliances of all nature. The ammunition assigned to the ship for transport was stored primarily in No. 1 hold, although additional quantities in containers were also loaded on the sports deck forward of the funnel, near what was normally the kennel. Equipment too large for convenient stowage or which might be needed quickly for off-loading by helicopters ended up on the open decks aft, on the raised boat deck, and on what was left of the upper deck. This included landrovers, trailers, helicopter parts, fuel, and rations. The combination of high-octane aviation fuel and ammunition in containers on open decks with the possibility of an Exocet missile attack was hair raising, but virtually no location on the QE2 offered much security against an attack.

In manning the ship for the voyage to the war zone, Cunard sought volunteers. Approximately 650 were chosen out of over 1,000 who had stepped forward. Finally, after eight whirlwind days of creating a fighting unit from the chaos of conversion, the QUEEN ELIZABETH 2 was ready to receive her most important military cargo. Preparation parties arrived on the afternoon of May 11 and the formal embarkation of troops began at 0545 hours on May 12, with regimental bands on hand to pipe the men aboard. Not unexpectedly, a large number of high officials wished to see the QUEEN off. Representing the owners were Lord Matthews and Ralph Bahna, president of Cunard Line. A selection of military brass saw their compatriots off, including an admiral and four generals plus staff. Finally, John Nott, minister for defense in the British government, arrived at 1430 hours for a quick tour of the bridge and a short address to the troops. The QUEEN had on board approximately 3,000 men of the Fifth Infantry Brigade comprising units of the Scots Guards, the Welsh Guards, and the Gurkha Rifles, in addition to naval personnel and her own crew. Departure time was scheduled for 1600 hours, and at 1603

Certainly one of the most impressive views of the QUEEN ELIZABETH 2 ever taken is this one from a Sea King helicopter as it circles the huge liner in the South Atlantic and begins an approach to the stern landing area.

hours the QE2's siren heralded the fact that all wires and ropes were clear fore and aft. With the tugs ALBERT, CALSHOT, and CLAUSENTUM fast forward and ROMSEY and BROCKENHURST fast astern, the 67,000-ton liner–troopship under the command of Captain Peter Jackson slowly headed upriver to turn. This was achieved within 23 minutes in spite of force 4/5 south-southeasterly winds, and the QUEEN ELIZABETH 2 proceeded to sea, past the terminal bearing her name, which was crowded with family and well wishers, to the wail of a Scottish bagpipe rendering "Scotland the Brave."

The departure was majestic, but not without anxiety. The routine maintenance on two of the three boilers still had not been completed on schedule, but, because of the enormous wartime propaganda value of an on-schedule departure, it was decided that the ship should sail on time. She would then drop anchor in the Channel and the maintenance could be completed by the ship's own staff under the leadership of the chief engineer, John Grant. The pilot, Captain Peter Driver, was far from pleased as he tried to maneuver his contrary charge with one-third power in winds that increased to force 7. The tug ALBERT remained in constant attendance, just in case there was any unforeseen trouble.

The QUEEN has three massive boilers as part of her propulsion machinery, and she can do up to 30 knots on all three, around 21 knots on two, but much less, 6–10 knots, on only one. With only one-third of her boilers in service, the ship was not capable of sudden stops or quick maneuvers, let alone much speed. While in port for an overnight stay or longer, only one boiler normally would be in use.

As the QUEEN ELIZABETH 2 steamed slowly down the Eastern Solent, passing Cowes and the coast of the Isle of Wight, the helicopter landing pads received their first baptism as two Sea King helicopters from the Royal Naval Air Station at Culdrose, Cornwall, which had previously flown to Portsmouth, made their cautious approach and touched down in Number Two and Three positions aft. The Number One position was on the forward pad on the bow. The first Sea King was piloted by Lieutenant Commander Hugh Clark, R.N., and the two were part of the 825th Naval Air Squadron. The helicopters were speedily secured in their appointed positions for the voyage, with their rotors folded back. As one Cunard officer commented, "it all appeared so practised and proficient that one would imagine we had been doing it for years."

The QUEEN anchored for the night, as planned, along the Isle of Wight, but away from curious onlookers. Early in the morning the tug BUSTLER brought still more stores on a quick trip, being alongside and away between 0120 and 0130 hours. Matters certainly looked much better by breakfast on May 13, and shortly after 0900 hours the order was given to "stand by engines." The anchor was weighed and to everyone's relief full power was soon available on the boilers.

The most dramatic part of the training sessions as the QUEEN ELIZABETH 2 steamed southward was the Sea King helicopter takeoff and landing exercises, which always drew an admiring crowd. The pilots found the aft landing pads required some time for familiarization. The landing pad guide lines ultimately were extended to the sides of the ship in order to increase visibility.

The safety of all on board was the prime concern of the QE2's officers, as well as the various military staffs. Shortly after getting underway on May 13 and before the Isle of Wight had dropped from view, the first full-scale boat drill was held at 1030 hours for the 3,000 troops. All lifeboats were swung out to the normal embarkation level so that everyone could see the full procedure. It was immediately evident that some reassignment of troops and mustering stations would have to occur because, as one officer said, "we had never had to cope with so many people before." The Gurkhas had been given accommodations on Five Deck because it was the most stable place on the liner. They supposedly were not immune to motion sickness. However, they decided that they should be proficient in reaching their assigned lifeboat from their cabins in pitch darkness. Therefore they blindfolded themselves and held their own lifeboat drills until they were satisfied with their ability to find their way around the great liner in total darkness. The confusion of the first day sorted itself out with the able assistance of Regimental Sergeant Major Hunt, whose voice could rival the QE2's foghorn for carrying power. Each muster station had an officer or NCO in charge, and each group of twenty-five men had a designated leader. In a real emergency each group of twenty-five would be directed to a lifeboat or a raft that already would have been swung out into the embarkation position by the ship's crew. Additional survival lectures and boat drills became part of each and every day's routine.

The principal job for the afternoon of the first day at sea was to experiment with at-sea replenishment of the QUEEN's fuel bunkers. She sailed from Southampton with 5,969 tons of fuel oil, but that was, in fact, barely enough to get her to the destination in the South Atlantic. Somewhere and somehow much more fuel would be needed. The QUEEN headed south to a

One of the most important reasons for requisitioning the QE2 was her ability to deliver physically fit troops and pilots to the war zone. Constant exercise routines with different groups went on throughout the day as the ship steamed south. Soldiers exercised in full kit so that their training and conditioning would make them fit for whatever challenges might materialize.

Helicopters are engaged on exercises while the QE2 steams along at full speed. Note the presence of trucks parked forward of the helicopter landing pads on the deck of the troopship.

The installation of a .5 Browning machine gun on each of the wings of the bridge may have given solace to some, but few were deluded about the ability of the huge liner–troopship to fight off a determined attack.

rendezvous point in the Channel with the Royal Fleet Auxiliary (RFA) tanker GREY ROVER. The afternoon also brought a special test of helicopter handling when the decision was made to transfer two soldiers, one with severe appendicitis and the other with an injured foot, to a shore hospital. At 1745 hours the helicopter took off for Treliske Hospital, Truro, with two patients, a doctor, and Jane Yelland, the senior nurse on the QE2, who returned five hours later thrilled with the experience. Those returning on the helicopter also brought every last copy of newspapers covering the war and the QE2's departure they could lay their hands on. These were greatly appreciated by their shipmates.

With the departure of the helicopter the QE2 made rendezvous with the tanker GREY ROVER, which approached from astern on the starboard side and fired a rocket line across to the troopship. The lightweight rocket line was attached to a second, intermediate line, which was attached to the "messenger." The two ships took up position about 150 feet apart, and a distance line was run across from the two forecastles. GREY ROVER had the responsibility for station keeping in a reversal of the traditional refueling roles. Approximately 100 soldiers took up position on Two Deck near the baggage door, which had been modified for fuel replenishment, and they took up the slack in the "messenger" and then pulled over the 8-inch flexible fuel line. With great difficulty this feat was achieved and the hose was connected to the

As dawn broke on May 28, those on the QE2 had their first view of Cumberland Bay, South Georgia, with the CANBERRA, dubbed the "Great White Whale," by her troops at anchor nearby. The 45,000-ton P&O liner would see a great deal of service in the South Atlantic before her return to Britain.

QE2's new bunker line, permitting the system to be tested by the passage of several tons of oil from the tanker to the QUEEN's bunkers. With the success of the experiment, the line was cleared, disconnected, and paid back out to GREY ROVER for retrieval. Since the refueling system was workable, the giant Cunarder could go anywhere and remain at sea indefinitely. As the two ships peeled away from each other, their horns thundered the traditional three-blast salute. In this instance the salute marked a job well done.

The QUEEN ELIZABETH 2 proceeded south, avoiding the normal sea-lanes on a 3,000-mile track toward Freetown, Sierra Leone. The second day out a French "Atlantic" reconnaissance plane buzzed the liner and wished her well. Thereafter it was felt that security from any sea-based unit was probably complete, although the problem of "spy satellites" makes all precautions under cloudless skies somewhat questionable against an enemy with such capability. Various news media quoted American intelligence reports as confirming that at least some of the twelve Soviet radar, photographic, and communication satellites were being used in a search for the liner as she steamed south. In a television interview former chief of naval operations Admiral Elmo Zumwalt said that he fully expected the Argentinians to make an attempt to destroy the QE2. "It is one big fat target," the admiral said.

The troops on the QUEEN ELIZABETH 2 were obsessed with physical fitness from the very beginning, both for the need to remain fit and as a means of reducing nervous energy. Every unit was given an assigned time period for jogging around the boat deck, starting at 0630 hours. All day long some of the 3,000 troops went around and around the boat deck, and the noise of hundreds of men in full kit and boots jogging around the open deck was deafening. Some Cunard staff began to hate the whole process with a passion, since the noise was omnipresent and thunderous. Within a short time the vibration from thousands of heavy footfalls began to lift the caulking right out of the teak deck. Streamers of caulking were everywhere, and, long after the QUEEN returned to commercial service, it was still lifting out in many areas.

Some of the ammunition on the ship was intended for firing practice, and this daily routine commenced on May 15. Bags of garbage made the best targets, but strong protests had to be lodged on occasions against random shots that destroyed railings. Every part of the ship was utilized for some form of training. Giant wall maps of the Falklands and the South Atlantic were spread across the Blue Staircase wall, where the tapestries of the launching of the QUEEN previously had hung. A newfound interest in South Atlantic geography was noted on the part of passers-by. The church service on Sunday morning, May 16, was well attended in the theater, with Captain Peter Jackson presiding.

Another daily routine as the QUEEN steamed southward was flying practice for the crews of the Sea King helicopters. From Friday, May 14, onward, several hours a day were devoted to this, in part because no one

A potentially dangerous load of ammunition leaves the flight deck of the QUEEN from the Number One Landing Pad, which had been constructed over the capstans on the foredeck of the QE2. Ammunition was off-loaded from the QE2 by helicopters as long as daylight and visibility permitted.

113

A dusting of snow blanketed the flight decks of the QUEEN ELIZABETH 2 on her second day at Grytviken, South Georgia. Grafitti instantaneously appeared in the new-fallen snow on the flight decks of the QE2, as few could resist the impulse to be creative.

actually knew where they would be required to disembark the troops or in what manner the disembarkation might be accomplished. Some of the pilots from the new 825th Squadron had never flown on and off a merchant ship before, even if their expertise in basic flying was unquestioned. Every ship is different, and even the veteran pilots of naval maneuvers had to learn where the air pockets and downdrafts would add extra challenges to landing on the QUEEN. It was necessary to practice not only fore and aft landings, but also athwartship touchdowns. If both the aft landing pads were in use at once, then one helicopter might come in from one direction while the other employed a different flight approach. The Number One landing position forward of the bridge in some ways was the most difficult of all because of air currents slamming into the front of the huge ship and being deflected upward and sideways, while the bow area also would be subject to more pitching. As one Cunard Officer commented, "one can appreciate that to land on a heaving deck in rough, rainy weather, with a ship doing 25 knots, would be difficult enough; however, to land sideways is a whole new ball game." The goal had to be to keep the ship in one's mind as a solid landing pad, match speed with her, maintain position, and ignore the millions of tons of water rushing by the hull. The South Atlantic would provide an icy grave for anyone forgetting their priorities, and no one wanted that!

After six days at sea at 0900 hours on Tuesday, May 18 the Cape Sierra Leone Light was sighted, and pilots Kenokai and Jones boarded. By 1145 hours all lines fore and aft were secure and the QUEEN was alongside a berth for what would be the last time in three weeks. The passage from Southampton to Freetown had taken 5 days, 1 hour, 24 minutes over a distance of 2,956 miles and had been accomplished at 24.35 knots. The engines, even at that economical reduced speed, had consumed 1,919 tons of oil, leaving 4,050 in the bunkers, so that 1,867 tons were taken on board, as well as additional water and supplies. The stop at Freetown was a calculated risk but it meant that the QUEEN could proceed to her destination without danger of running low on fuel and using the pipeline system. Furthermore, security was such that the QUEEN ELIZABETH 2 slipped in and out of Freetown unnoticed by the world's press. With the tug SENA forward and INTERMAN aft, the liner sailed from the West Coast of Africa with her bunkers topped up. The destination for this leg of the trip south was Ascension Island. The late-night departure from Freetown featured as crew and troop entertainment a film on deck. The scene of a large military troopship showing a film on deck during a hot tropical night as the ship sailed from an African port took some viewers back forty years to another conflict.

One of the most critical tasks on the QUEEN ELIZABETH 2 after leaving Freetown was the creation of a total ship blackout. In the words of Captain J. James, R.N., senior naval officer on the QUEEN, the giant liner had to be converted from "the brightest star on the ocean, to the darkest." There are an awful lot of portholes on the QE2, and hundreds of large floor-to-ceiling public room windows. At the same time, in tackling the problem there was no desire to apply black paint everywhere if anything else would do. Black plastic, such as that used in garbage bags, came to the rescue for temporary service. The four regular carpenters of the QUEEN under the able leadership of Bill Bailey cut out and fashioned forms from which black plastic could be cut in a variety of shapes. Two army officers were assigned to each deck to supervise the securing of the black plastic over the portholes. The result was satisfactory. The large public room windows were parceled out to various work groups who also covered them with sheets of plastic. By concentrated effort, the whole of the job was accomplished in three days. It was found that in the tropics the black plastic had a tendency to crinkle when subjected to the sun's rays and that the blackened windows created a greenhouse effect within the QE2 that substantially taxed the air conditioning, but at least she was darkened. Night helicopter flights were made to inspect the handiwork

The QE2 is shrouded in an icy fog in Cumberland Bay East, South Georgia, as trawlers work energetically to remove men and supplies from the liner. The photograph was taken from one of the QUEEN's launches taking a small party of Cunard personnel to see the whaling station at Grytviken.

An unidentified hulk in Grytviken Harbor provides a picturesque scene in a monochrome setting. The principal human settlement from the days of the whaling industry in South Georgia was Grytviken, although the site had been abandonned as a working community. The spark that started the war occurred when Argentinian workers, brought here to dismantle the whaling station for scrap, raised the Argentine flag and thereby produced a chain reaction which resulted in hostilities. On the right of the scene in the distance is the conning tower of the sunken Argentine submarine SANTA FE.

and it was found that from a mile away the ship was difficult to spot, except for the navigation lights, which were not used after Ascension Island.

Ascension Island lay only a day and a half's steaming from Freetown for the QE2. Captain Jackson's orders were to stay 25 miles away from the island in case of unfriendly surveillance. There was some irritation at finding on the morning of Thursday, May 20, that the liner was sighted by a Russian trawler, PRIMORYE, heavily equipped with sophisticated radar and known in intelligence circles as an Alien Intelligence Gatherer (AIG). The Russian ship ultimately departed, and rendezvous was made with H.M.S. DUMBARTON CASTLE, a Royal Navy North Sea and Oil Rig protection vessel with helicopter-handling capabilities. The Sea King helicopters of the QE2 shuttled stores and men from DUMBARTON CASTLE, which maintained station off the starboard side of the liner. Between 1330 and 1600 hours helicopter operations were completed, but the QE2 steamed around at 20 knots waiting for Major-General J. J. Moore, Commander Land Forces, and his command staff who were flying out from the United Kingdom to Ascension for rendezvous with the ship. On Friday, May 21, General Moore landed on the QUEEN while a constant stream of helicopters brought over 200 tons of stores and 10 tons of mail, some of which bore postmarks only four days old.

At Ascension Island there was some very impressive flying, with at times three helicopters stacked up off the stern waiting to land supplies. The Royal Navy flight coordinator on the bridge, Lieutenant Roger Bevan, R.N., and his men worked like demons to make sure everything went smoothly, while the deck and landing pad crews moved tons of cargo under arduous and crowded conditions. At times even the Number One spot, forward, was used, but only by the Sea King pilots, who had more experience in flying sideways at the same speed as the QE2. On one occasion a Sea King pilot also landed an underslung load on the aft deck of the QE2 as she executed a neat 180-degree turn. One aid to landing was modified for greater visibility and safety when the white cross marks were extended all the way to the side of the ship in order to avoid periodic blind spots near touchdown. The pilot of a Chinook based on Ascension also showed impressive flying skill when he brought his big twin-rotored helicopter level with the bridge and kept pace for a while so that his crew could take pictures of the QUEEN slicing through the South Atlantic. The big Chinook was a breathtaking as well as a humorous sight, with flight crew sprouting out of every available crevice, including the tailgate, with cameras. As a bit of "I can too" bravado, the Chinook turned 90 degrees and flew sideways, keeping pace with the bridge of the mammoth ship.

Among the "STUFT" (Ships Taken Up From Trade) steaming toward the war zone were the passenger ferries BALTIC FERRY and NORDIC FERRY, which were a day or so ahead when the QE2 reached Ascension, and the container vessel ATLANTIC CAUSEWAY, which was a day behind. All those ships had additional troops, pilots, helicopters, and stores belonging to the Fifth Infantry

The morning sunlight brilliantly lights one of the snow-capped peaks of South Georgia as seen from the after deck of the QUEEN ELIZABETH 2 in Cumberland Bay. A few crew members briefly stop to admire the breathtaking beauty of the sight.

Brigade that the QUEEN was transporting. The decision was made to transfer some critical supplies from the ATLANTIC CAUSEWAY to the QE2, and a rendezvous was made during the night. The flights were postponed until the afternoon of Saturday, May 22, around 1300 hours, and again all went smoothly. No sooner was the decision made for one flight than it seemed that several trips were needed to complete the appointed tasks.

On Sunday, May 23, as the QUEEN ELIZABETH 2 headed southward on the last leg of her outward voyage, the radar was turned off and the ship was electronically silenced. Modern radar is a great boon to navigation, but in wartime a dead giveaway as to the location of a ship. Therefore the officers on the bridge had the clock turned back on them some forty years, and the importance of a sharp watch was never more critical. From dawn to dusk military lookouts were posted on the bridge wings as well as near the funnel. The watertight doors on decks 6, 7, and 8 had been shut earlier, but as the ship steamed closer to the war zone all other watertight doors were closed as a safety precaution.

The closer to the war the QE2 came, the keener attention was paid to the news. Before May 21 not too much happened, but after that, with the landing on San Carlos by the British on the 22nd and with the news of the successful Argentinian strikes against H.M.S. ARDENT, ANTELOPE, and CONVENTRY, as well as the ATLANTIC CONVEYOR, the war was suddenly a reality. To those listening on the QUEEN the air raids against British ships seemed incessant, even if the Argentinians were taxing their men and planes to the limit. The loss of the ATLANTIC CONVEYOR, a Cunard ship, caused particular concern for those who had friends on her, since the loss of life was substantial.

On May 24 two platforms on the bridge wings were finished to hold the mounting for .5 Browning machine guns. The Browning machine guns could fire around 800 rounds a minute. In addition, 7.62-millimeter general-purpose machine guns and Blow Pipe Air Defense missiles were located in a few strategic positions. These were the only armaments carried for the QUEEN's own protection. The firing exercises added to the din, although there were fewer helicopter flights in order to conserve fuel. Some exuberant marksman managed to damage the No. 5 raft-launching davit fall wire, which had to be replaced, while bullet holes in the forward rails met with strong protests by the Cunard representatives at the daily afternoon conferences.

By noon on May 26 the ship was in position, latitude 47°59′ South, 25°20′ West, and the air temperature, which had been steadily falling, was now 5 degrees Celsius. Soon it would be below zero with a wind chill factor far lower than that, and cold weather gear was in demand all around. The troops continued their routines in spite of the cold. The Cunard crew was given a briefing by Captain James and Brigadier Tony Wilson in the theater, during which the military officers explained some of the problems and dangers that had been or might be experienced. Brigadier Wilson concluded his talk by

The famed Gurkhas of the British Army made up one of the contingents traveling south on the QE2. They had accommodations deep in the liner on Five Deck and practiced reaching their lifeboat stations blindfolded in order to be prepared for any eventuality.

The grave of the intrepid British Antarctic explorer Sir Ernest Shackleton lies
in the little wind-swept cemetery at
Grytviken. Many naval visitors have
paid their respects at the site and left
their ship emblems in tribute.

Trawlers nestle against the side of the
QUEEN ELIZABETH 2 awaiting the
opportunity to take on troops or supplies.
The North Sea car ferry NORLAND can
be seen in the distance through the fog.

stating that the Cunard crew members were the only volunteers on this voyage and were thus well respected by the troops. The good feelings that resulted from Brigadier Wilson's talk went a long way to iron out any differences that might have occurred and made the crew members much more aware of the dangers that lay ahead. However, as one Cunard officer commented, "it was too late to turn around now!" No one was so inclined.

Efforts were made at continuous entertainment to break the tedium and tension of the voyage. Shortly after the departure from Southampton there had been a meeting of the QUEEN's Wardroom, and all the R.N. officers attached to the ship for the duration of requisition were elected as temporary members. The Cunard officers and their military counterparts endeavored to host each other, and on several occasions all the women on the ship were invited to the Wardroom for drinks. About thirty women went to war on the QUEEN ELIZABETH 2, including Linda Kitson, a professional artist, who was commissioned by the Imperial War Museum to make drawings of the task force. On one evening Brigadier Wilson had planned an on-deck party, but the blackout squashed the plans, so it was held in the Q4 Bar instead. Since the principal entertainment involved ten minutes of Gurkha bagpipes followed by the fifes and drums of the Welsh Guards and the pipers of the Scots Guards, almost everyone emerged from the experience nearly deaf. One officer described the program as "excellent stuff, but a little hard on the ears within the comparatively small room." No one was so impolite to comment that nothing short of the Edinburgh Castle Esplanade was probably large enough for such a musical program.

May 26 had also placed the QUEEN near enough to the active war zone that she began to zigzag rather than just steering variable courses as before. During the night of May 26–27 mist settled in around midnight and visibility was reduced substantially while the presence of ice became ever more ominous. The situation in the darkness rapidly deteriorated to such a critical level that the danger from the numerous icebergs was considered far greater than that from hostile forces. Captain Jackson had gone to the bridge as the fog settled in. He consulted with the naval authorities as the QE2 was forced to reduce speed and to weave in and out between the giant bergs. Finally, in spite of the danger of revealing the ship's position, the radar was turned on at 0340 hours. The possibility of the QUEEN becoming trapped by icebergs or colliding with one was a more imminent risk than discovery by the enemy. During the next 6 hours many icebergs of monstrous proportions suddenly loomed out of the misty darkness, and at one time over 100 bergs large enough to be seen by the radar were on the scan. Each of those great masses of ice could sink a ship. The largest of the gigantic bergs was over a mile long—six times the length of the QUEEN—and at 300 feet high must have weighed in at several million tons—many times the liner's gross tonnage. Captain Jackson described the time on the bridge as he took his charge through the ice field as the most harrowing experience he had had in nearly forty years at sea. With visibility less than a mile and sometimes even less than that, expert seamanship and the legendary Cunard luck saw the QUEEN ELIZABETH 2 through the icefield. As dawn broke, the iceberg danger was past, although one huge berg could still be seen 7 miles from the QUEEN, soaring above the low lying mist and probably towering 200–300 feet above the rolling South Atlantic. It was so huge that it looked like the Cliffs of Dover, while another appeared like cathedral spires rising from the turbulent sea. As the sun rose, the icebergs reflected a rainbow of colors in magnificent shades of red, orange, and yellow. After what the individuals on the bridge of the QUEEN had just been through, it was difficult for some not to think of 1912, of another great luxury liner, and another iceberg.

A rendezvous with H.M.S. ANTRIM was planned for noon on Thursday, May 27, in order to transfer Major-General Moore and Brigadier Wilson with their advanced headquarters. Before Brigadier Wilson left the QE2, he penned a parting message for publication in the "5th Infantry Brigade/QE2 News" that summed up the role of the soldiers and the liner to that date:

> Very shortly we shall all transfer to other ships off South Georgia and start on the last phase of our move to the Falkland Islands. It looks as if the Brigade will be there about 1st June, that is early next week.

The fastest means of transferring large numbers of troops from the QE2 to the other waiting transports was by the trawlers, and one is shown leaving the side of the liner. The trawlers also worked relentlessly around the clock trans-shipping stores brought by the QUEEN to other waiting vessels.

Once there, we shall join 3 Commando Brigade. We shall sort ourselves out; and then start joint operations to recapture the islands.

Orders will be given out on landing. It is too early yet to issue a detailed plan, for it would be bound to change over the course of the next 5 days.

This is the final issue of this newspaper, and to the Master and ship's company of QE2 I would say 'Thank you' for the way you have looked after us on this voyage. We have come to know you well, we admire you, and we shall always be proud that we sailed with you in your magnificent ship.

To the Brigade I would simply say this: "We shall start earning our pay as a team shortly; and we are in this game to win!"

Major-General Moore and Brigadier Wilson left the QE2 on schedule for the rendezvous with H.M.S. ANTRIM—a remarkable achievement, considering the ice of the previous night. The general and his staff went by helicopter, but two of the QUEEN's launches were used to transport the brigadier and the 5th Brigade Party. The goal was to have General Moore rendezvous with Admiral Sandy Woodward at sea en route to the Falkland Islands so that additional plans could be formulated. The sea was calm when the QE2 launched her boats, but the swell was several feet high and this made disembarkation alongside ANTRIM treacherous. One warrant officer suffered a broken leg when it became trapped between the launch and H.M.S ANTRIM. The war was over for him, and he returned to the QUEEN's hospital by helicopter. The recovery of the QE2's launches proved difficult because of the swell. Considerable stress was placed on the falls as the weight of the launch came on them quite suddenly when the swell subsided.

When the QE2 had neared H.M.S. ANTRIM, it was evident that she already had seen considerable action both in South Georgia and the East Falklands.

After leaving South Georgia, the QUEEN ELIZABETH 2 encountered gale-force winds that made refueling operations with the fleet oiler BAYLEAF treacherous. By June 2 the QUEEN was down to less than 1,000 tons of fuel (less than 2 days' supply at full speed), and it was imperative to attempt transferring the precious fuel from the tanker to the liner.

Her exterior was distinctly weather beaten and the battles she had fought were highlighted by the line of cannon shell holes down her sides. The Seacat missile launcher was out of commission as the result of an unexploded Argentinian bomb that had lodged itself in the missile magazine. Fortunately the bomb had been defused before it could explode or the ANTRIM would have had her stern ripped off.

At 1804 hours on May 27, Right Whale Rocks, South Georgia, was 4½ miles away, but visibility was virtually nil; the short South Atlantic winter day had already given way to night and there was thick fog. As the ship approached the planned anchorage, the cable was walked back two shackles. By 1922 hours the vessel was safely at anchor approximately 1 mile from Grytviken. The passage from Freetown, Sierra Leone, had been over a distance of 5,025 miles and had taken 8 days, 20 hours, 12 minutes, with an average speed of 23.9 knots in spite of ice. During that period the QUEEN's engines also had consumed 3,570 tons of her precious fuel. South Georgia represented as much of the war zone as the liner would see, since other vessels would tend to the transfer of her critical troops to the Falkland Islands, themselves some 200 miles to the west. The QUEEN's anchorage was in Cumberland Bay East near the old whaling station of Grytviken, the origin of the whole conflict.

Among the other vessels in Cumberland Bay East was the P&O liner CANBERRA, the North Sea ferry NORLAND, and H.M.S. ENDURANCE, as well as a number of trawlers outfitted as mine sweepers that had arrived from England just the previous day. They served as transports for the troops from the QE2 to the other ships. Soon after anchoring, Captain Barker, R.N., of H.M.S. ENDURANCE and the senior naval officer, Captain C. Burr, R.N., of the CANBERRA came on board to meet with the S.N.O. QE2, Captain James, and the senior military officers present. The meeting held in the Queen Mary Suite was to agree on a plan for disembarkation. The communications blackout had seen the development of two alternative plans that now needed to be resolved. Those on the QE2 wanted to start unloading the cargo immediately, since it was going to take at least 48 hours. Those coming on board wanted the troops to begin transferring immediately, with the movement of cargo to go forward simultaneously. All involved had well thought-out arguments that, as befitted strong personalities, were expressed in firm straightforward opinions. Eventually agreement was reached and about 700 troops commenced disembarkation at 2345 hours for transfer to CANBERRA and NORLAND. The requisitioned British trawlers did yeomen's service, transporting the troops in the dark between the blackened ships. H.M.S. LEEDS CASTLE, sister ship to the DUMBARTON CASTLE at Ascension and one of the North Sea vessels, was the first of the smaller ships to try to come alongside the QE2 in the darkness. The QE2 was visible at only 100 feet, and the approach of the LEEDS CASTLE was foiled when her mast hit the bridge

RAS piping was installed on Two Deck amidships leading down to the liner's fuel tanks. The critically needed fuel supplies in the thousands of tons came gushing in through these pipes and descended through the ship to the bunkers.

wing of the QUEEN as she tried to maneuver forward to be underneath No. I hatch. The CORDELLA, one of the converted trawlers, was the first vessel to make it alongside successfully. She was one of five trawlers requisitioned and outfitted as the new 11th Mine Countermeasures Squadron. Her sister ships in the squadron were the NORTHELLA, FARNELLA, PICT, and JUNELLA. They were manned by Royal Navy officers and ratings and adapted to act as mine sweepers in the Falklands, but they had many other uses.

Despite the late hour, the soldiers were in good spirits. The trawlers came alongside the QE2 with difficulty because of the low visibility. Security dictated that no lights were to be used. No doubt the liner and the trawlers lost some paint during the night. A start was made on discharging No. I hatch, but it was just too difficult in the blackness, and the bulk of the work had to be put off until daylight.

The first real view of Cumberland Bay East and South Georgia came with the dawn on May 28. Snow-capped mountains spawned glaciers that flowed to the sea, forming numerous small icebergs in the waters of the bay. Discharge of the troops and stores began at 0800 hours with helicopters and trawlers. The work proceeded quickly because of the uncertain weather conditions and the desire of all concerned to get the QE2 out of the anchorage as expeditiously as possible. The transfer of baggage, equipment, and personnel continued all day by helicopter and trawlers. The Admiralty tug TYPHOON also assisted in transfers to the waiting NORLAND. It soon appeared that, even with all the smaller vessels working full-time, not all of the troops would make it to their assigned ships on schedule. One of the 7th Gurkha officers asked if he could use the QE2's launches to transport his men to the North Sea ferry. This request was granted, and just before noon the QUEEN's launches began to load the short Gurkhas and their nearly overwhelming bulk of equipment. When the boats reached the NORLAND, they found that she had no pontoon alongside and that her hatch, normally used for disembarking cars, was 8 feet above the water and higher than the Gurkhas were tall by a very good measure. There is no question that the Gurkhas are among the finest fighting troops in the world but this represented a very substantial challenge. The troops could not even see the NORLAND's deck, let alone reach it, from the QE2's launches. The solution was to use the cab of the launch plus a good boost to get the soldiers on their way.

Snow started to fall on May 29 at 0400 hours, and by daybreak it had settled everywhere, blanketing South Georgia with a couple of inches. The snow was very beautiful to see, but treacherous to work in. Nevertheless, more than 100 tons of cargo still had to go. This was loaded into trawlers for transfer to H.M.S. STROMNESS, which had arrived shortly before noon. The Sea King helicopters had been permanently transferred to CANBERRA the day before. As matters were being tidied up there was time to think of others, and a QE2 launch was sent ashore to take some Cunard and army personnel

The homecoming to Southampton on June 11 was spectacular, with welcoming escorts in the Solent. The survivors from the ARDENT, ANTELOPE, and COVENTRY lined the decks of the QUEEN ELIZABETH 2 to greet Her Majesty Queen Elizabeth, the Queen Mother, on the Royal Yacht.

for a visit and to bring some of the Royal Marines who were garrisoning the bleak base at Grytviken back to the liner for lunch and a much appreciated break. When the Cunard group reached shore, the Captain in charge took them around the old whaling station. Nearby was the wreck of the Argentinian submarine SANTA FE, which was sunk in shallow water with the conning tower still above the water. The whaling station had been closed for twenty years and most of the timber buildings showed the ravages of numerous South Atlantic hurricanes, but the church was well preserved. The tradition of the island was that anyone remaining on South Georgia for any period of time repaired and maintained the church. Chris Haughton, one of the QE2's second officers, walked ahead toward the church, and as the others approached they were astounded to be greeted by Bach's Toccata and Fugue in D floating heavenward from the old pump organ. The impression was breathtaking to the visitors. Outside of town near the shore was the old cemetery with the grave of the famous Antarctic explorer Sir Ernest Shackleton which was decorated with the crested shields of visiting ships in tribute to the gallant adventurer. Some of those who went ashore brought back harpoon heads as souvenirs, and Wendy Marshall, a nurse who was in the visiting party, lugged back a hunk of whalebone for the ship's doctor. The thirty young marines who visited the QE2 also received a surprise shipment of mail from home, the first in some weeks.

During the afternoon of May 29 some 640 survivors of H.M.S. ARDENT, CONVENTRY, and ANTELOPE were transferred to the QE2. The QUEEN thus became the largest hospital ship in the world. Many of the survivors of the lost Royal Navy vessels had little more than the clothes on their backs, and some of those were ragged. These men had been through the fiery furnace of war and they were a very stern-faced and determined group of Royal Navy sailors. The officers and crew of the QE2 did their best to make them feel welcome and to assist in the unwinding process from the high level of tension these warriors had endured. Most of the survivors could be accommodated in normal cabins, but the hospital of the QUEEN was soon filled with the more critical casualties, who were, according to the medical staff, very lucky to be alive.

The barometer was falling steadily throughout the day and the weather was giving cause for concern. The swell coming in the entrance to Cumberland Bay East caused the QUEEN to yaw wildly. This made it increasingly difficult for the trawlers to come alongside safely. The port gangway and pontoon were damaged beyond further use by the buffeting they received. In order to minimize the exposure of the smaller vessels, the QE2 weighed anchor and turned to create a lee shore for the last disembarkation of troops. Meanwhile, during the afternoon a report was received that the tanker BRITISH WYE was under attack 400 miles due north. An Argentinian aircraft dropped a series of bombs that fortunately missed. The incident was a

Her Majesty Queen Elizabeth, the Queen Mother, stands on the aft deck of the BRITANNIA to welcome the troops home.

particular cause for concern, as the tanker was a considerable distance from the mainland and to the north of South Georgia. By deduction, this meant that the QE2 was in range and a sitting duck while anchored at Cumberland Bay. (Later it was learned that the Argentinians had used a Boeing 707 with a very substantial cruising range to survey the South Atlantic at 18,000 feet searching for the QUEEN ELIZABETH 2.) That afternoon it was deemed judicious to get the huge liner out of Cumberland Bay East in order to reduce her vulnerability. She put out to sea at 1727 hours with 60 tons of ammunition still remaining on board.

The QUEEN increased speed to 18 knots and headed into the icefield that had been so terrifying on the way south. By 1930 hours the liner passed the first of the giant bergs in darkness, but the feeling this time was that night and the ice would make it all the more difficult for the Argentinians to find the ship. Furthermore, within 2½ hours the QE2 was clear of the main icefield and increased speed to 25 knots, with more in reserve should danger strike. Although no one knew it, she was on her way home.

On Sunday, May 30, Captain Jackson held the Sunday service with Captain James reading the special lesson and prayers. The weather deteriorated substantially, with rough seas slamming against the ship and heavy swells churning the South Atlantic. Even some strong-willed souls felt moderate discomfiture from this weather, although the good news was that under such conditions the QUEEN could still maintain speed and stand a much better chance of escaping detection from hostile submarines and aircraft.

The fuel situation was becoming increasingly acute as night fell on May 31. Rendezvous was made with the R.F.A. tanker BAYLEAF, but conditions on Monday and Tuesday, June 1, had been too wicked for any attempt at fuel transfer. The arrangements on both days had to be canceled. By Wednesday, June 2, the options were severely reduced, with the giant liner down to less than 1,000 tons of fuel (1½ days steaming at full power).

Speed was reduced to 10 knots and course set at 300 degrees to facilitate pipeline connecting. The BAYLEAF came up on the QUEEN's starboard side shortly after 0900 hours and the pipe was secured by 0905 hours on the first try in a miracle of precision work under horrendous conditions. The two ships were rolling along, 150 feet apart, with the sea boiling between them. The violent movements of the ships at times made the hose appear to be almost horizontal. There was more than one near miss, and Captain Jackson grew a few more gray hairs as the fate of his ship was taken out of his hands once again. All day the two ships kept position, with the tanker captain having the additionally demanding responsibility of keeping station on the QUEEN ELIZABETH 2 rather than the other way around, as was normal when refueling takes place between naval vessels. At 1835 hours, after 12½ hours, the decision was made to cease refueling because the pipeline clearly was chaffing and night was descending fast. By that time the QUEEN had taken on board almost 3,834 tons of fuel, which would be sufficient to sustain operations quite

Following the return to Southampton on June 11, 1982, the QUEEN ELIZABETH 2 was returned to the Cunard Line. The restoration of the ship as a five-star passenger liner took place at Southampton in the huge dock originally built to accommodate the QUEEN MARY and QUEEN ELIZABETH. The ship is shown in dry dock during the reconditioning.

a while at 25 knots. The decision to stop replenishing was fortuitous—it was discovered that the joining shackle supporting the weight of the hose within the ship had almost worn away and would have given out in another few minutes.

Initially the feeling was that the survivors of the lost British ships would disembark at Ascension Island for the long flight home. Therefore the navy opted to give the QE2 a crew show to remember. Acts were assembled quickly and the Double Up–Double Down Room of the QE2 rang with raunchy jokes and hilarious nonstop routines as everyone unwound to the best medicine ever invented—laughter. There were few unaffected as the officers and sailors wound up the program with a rousing, full-throated rendering of "God Save the Queen!" A naval mess dinner was given by the resident naval party for the officers of the QE2 in the Princess Grill. Clothes were still at a premium, but spirit was not and the officers retired to the Queen's Grill Lounge for traditional mess games. Such levity served to break some of the strain for all concerned and to help those who had experienced the trauma of losing their ships regain stability and peace of mind.

On June 3 the orders were received from the ministry of defense to return to Southampton. The QUEEN ELIZABETH 2 had succeeded so well in her assignment that she was no longer required in the war zone and could best serve the Crown by bringing the survivors home. This news was received with mixed reactions. Many of the crew were emotionally prepared to spend at least two months away, and they felt that they had not participated enough in the cause. The CANBERRA, it seemed, had done so much more, and the crew of the QE2 were prepared to make additional sacrifices. Such was the esprit de corps. Yet, as Captain Jackson and others explained, the QUEEN ELIZABETH 2 had accomplished something that no other vessel could have by delivering the majority of the 5th Brigade to the war zone within two weeks, safe and sound.

On Friday, June 4, as the QUEEN neared Ascension Island, she rendezvoused with H.M.S. DUMBARTON CASTLE at 1500 hours and then turned her bow northward, leaving the South Atlantic behind. Six survivors of a helicopter crash departed the ship at Ascension with two severe casualties to be flown home, but the bulk of the survivors remained on board for the voyage home. Twenty-five tons of ammunition also were transferred by helicopter for potential use in the war. Good weather continued, and the operation was carried out smoothly. June 5 saw the normal morning lifeboat drill as the QUEEN steamed northward at 23.89 knots. The sea was moderate and the weather fair as a balmy cruise climate prevailed. A survivors' competition on June 8 for the title "Miss QE2" was won by a sailor with a beard, and daily sports competitions kept the troops active and occupied. One group from one of the lost ships even built a temporary pool on the aft deck. Nothing like ten days at sea on the QE2 to restore the health and minds of war-torn individuals, but the biggest thrill lay ahead.

The removal of the aft helicopter landing pads from the liner is underway in this dry dock photo. While reconstruction to prepare for the Falklands was accomplished in less than a week (May 5 to May 12, 1982), reconditioning consumed the better part of nine weeks (June 12 to August 7, 1982).

On June 6 a signal was received by Captain Jackson informing him that the liner would be returned to Cunard immediately upon her arrival in Southampton, but the refit was not expected to be completed until August 14—eight weeks later. The news also arrived and spread like wildfire through the ship that the QUEEN ELIZABETH 2 would be greeted in the Solent by the Royal Yacht BRITANNIA with Her Majesty Queen Elizabeth, the Queen Mother, on board to welcome them home. Therefore the "boys" had to be dressed properly. The "hands to flying stations" sounded yet again at 1540 hours on Thursday, June 10 and helicopters from the Royal Naval Station, Culdrose, Cornwall, landed with all sorts of gear for the 640 survivors of the ARDENT, COVENTRY, and ANTELOPE. A few important military personnel also arrived to give orders about secrecy and how to handle the press. At 1830 hours the QE2 passed Mounts Bay near Penzance, and by 2200 hours the helicopters lifted off for Culdrose once more while the liner steamed slowly up the Channel to her well-earned welcome home.

The timetable for the QUEEN ELIZABETH 2's arrival in her home port on June 11 was carefully orchestrated. Captain Driver, the QUEEN's frequent pilot, boarded at 0848 hours and the Needles were past at 0900 hours. Admiral Sir John Fieldhouse, commander in chief of the Royal Navy, landed on board at 0800 hours and, after addresses to the crews and a press conference, he left by 0935 hours. Lord Matthews also arrived as the senior Cunard representative and made his way around the ship, speaking to personnel. Admiral Fieldhouse's use of the Q4 Nightclub for the press conference was one of the last official events held in that room which was subsequently transformed into the Club Lido. Following Admiral Fieldhouse's departure, the survivors of the ARDENT, COVENTRY, and ANTELOPE mustered on the upper deck aft (flight deck) as the QE2 slowly steamed up the Solent and BRITANNIA came into view with Her Majesty Queen Elizabeth, the Queen Mother, waving to the ship from the after deck of the yacht. All those on the QUEEN ELIZABETH 2 gave three resounding cheers to Her Majesty.

The exchange of radiograms between Her Majesty and Captain Jackson has been immortalized in two large silver plaques that now grace one of the lobbies of the liner bracketed by the standards of Queen Elizabeth II and Queen Elizabeth, the Queen Mother. The message sent to Captain Jackson read:

I AM PLEASED TO WELCOME YOU BACK AS QE2 RETURNS TO HOME WATERS AFTER YOUR TOUR OF DUTY IN THE SOUTH ATLANTIC. THE EXPLOITS OF YOUR OWN SHIP'S COMAPNY AND THE DEEDS OF VALOR OF THOSE WHO SERVED IN ANTELOPE, COVENTRY AND ARDENT HAVE BEEN ACCLAIMED THROUGHOUT THE LAND AND I AM PROUD TO ADD MY PERSONAL TRIBUTE.

(SIGNED)

ELIZABETH REGINA

QUEEN MOTHER

Captain Peter Jackson's reply was:

PLEASE CONVEY TO HER MAJESTY QUEEN ELIZABETH OUR THANKS FOR HER
KIND MESSAGE. CUNARD'S QUEEN ELIZABETH 2 IS PROUD TO HAVE BEEN OF
SERVICE TO HER MAJESTY'S FORCES.

As the QE2 passed the Fawley oil refinery, every tanker and vessel, great and
small, thundered, whistled, or shrieked a salute to the liner, filling the air with
the cacaphony normally reserved for a maiden voyage. Southampton Harbor
was crawling with small boats out to view the historic occasion of yet a third
"Queen liner" returning from a war. The QE2 was assisted to her berth by the
tugs ALBERT and CULVER forward and VENTNOR, CHALE, and CALSHOT aft. The
huge liner swung in the basin as people became visible out of the enormous
throng and all lines were made fast by 1156 hours, with the port side to the
QE2 terminal. Some of the QUEEN's officers took the opportunity to walk into
the Wardroom and watch their ship as she was being shown live on television.
A gangway was down within minutes, and the naval survivors walked ashore
over a red carpet, were handed red roses, and directed to a quiet area inside
the QE2 Terminal for a private reunion with their families. The QE2's own
crew disembarked via the forward gangway, where hundreds of happy family
members had gathered to greet them in a wild rush. It was a very emotional
day for everyone. The QUEEN ELIZABETH 2 was home safe and sound.

Passage from South Georgia to Southampton: 12 days, 12 hours, 18 minutes

Distance: 6,976 miles

Average speed: 23.23 knots

Fuel: 1,076 tons (remaining); 4,798 tons (consumed)

Arrival draught: 26 feet, 4 inches forward; 31 feet, 10 inches aft

Total distance steamed: Southampton to Southampton: 14,967 miles

Value of fuel at $180/ton: $1,851,660

---

CHAPTER SEVEN

*The Present
and Future Queen*

On August 7, 1982, the QUEEN ELIZABETH 2 put to sea for 24 hours of engine trials following her refit after service in the South Atlantic. It had taken only seven days to convert the QE2 into a troopship, but to restore her took the better part of nine weeks. Following the removal of the two helicopter pads, a considerable amount of structural restoration had to be carried out, as well as internal refurbishing.

The time that the government required to restore the ship gave Cunard a unique opportunity to make several improvements of their own. Among the new facilities installed was the Golden Door Spa. This has proved enormously popular with health- and weight-conscious travelers of all ages, and the idea ultimately was extended to other Cunard ships. The Queen's Grill was redesigned and the casino expanded and redecorated. The first stage of the new Club Lido was carried out, which involved the repositioning of the bar and the fitting of glass doors at the after end leading out onto the open deck. The results were striking and received many favorable comments.

Certainly the most noticeable change was in the color scheme of the liner. The dark-gray hull was repainted with a light pebble gray that was almost white, and the funnel was redone in the traditional Cunard red with the two black bands. The goal was to give the QE2 a new and exciting appearance after her return from trooping duties, and this certaintly was achieved. However, the pebble gray was terribly difficult to maintain in a pristine form, and no matter how careful the Moran tugs were in New York, the QUEEN always lost some of her paint. After a reasonable trial period in the new color scheme, it was decided to revert to the original dark gray. She was repainted in June 1983.

On August 15 the Pride of the British Merchant Fleet sailed from Southampton with a full complement of passengers destined for New York. Thousands of well wishers gave her a rousing send-off. Wessex helicopters flew overhead in salute, and a flotilla of small boats accompanied her out into the Channel. Prior to her departure Cunard chairman Lord Matthews hosted a reception on board. In his speech he stated that Cunard was delighted to have the QUEEN ELIZABETH 2 back in service and that it would take something like £200 million ($300 million) to replace her. The QUEEN, he said, was unique and, given existing commercial conditions, likely to remain so for the rest of her life. She was the last of the great transatlantic ocean liners.

At the end of the 1982 season Queen Elizabeth, the Queen Mother, paid a personal tribute to the liner when she visited the ship at Southampton on December 2, 1982. The Queen Mother toured the ship with Lord Matthews and Captain Peter Jackson and spoke to many members of the ship's company who had sailed to South Georgia. She presented a handsomely embossed plaque to the ship to commemorate the vessel's service in the Falkland campaign. The plaque records the messages exchanged between the Queen Mother and Captain Jackson while the QE2 was steaming past the Royal

The reconditioning of the QUEEN ELIZABETH 2 following her return from the Falklands is nearly completed. The most striking aspect of this was the repainting of the hull to pebble gray as part of her new image. In a rare situation astern of the 67,703-ton QE2 lies the 44,807-ton CANBERRA, the second largest passenger liner in the British Merchant Marine, which also was being reconditioned after service in the South Atlantic.

During the 1983 Great Pacific and Orient Odyssey Cruise the QUEEN ELIZABETH 2 lies off Moorea in one of the most beautiful tropical settings in the world.

Pristine in her new color scheme, the QUEEN ELIZABETH 2 returned to service in August 1982. In June 1983, the decision was made to return to a darker, gray hull that was substantially easier to maintain.

Yacht in the Solent on her return voyage. The plaque is now on display by the Royal Standards situated between the casino and the Theatre Bar on the upper deck.

In January 1983 the QUEEN ELIZABETH 2 set forth on her annual long cruise, which was called "The Great Pacific and Oriental Odyssey." The liner sailed from wintry New York to Florida and the Caribbean and then via the Panama Canal to the West Coast of Mexico and as far north as San Francisco before heading south toward the Tahitian Islands in the South Pacific and on toward New Zealand and Australia. One of the highlights of the 1983 Great Pacific and Oriental Odyssey was the maiden arrival of the QUEEN ELIZABETH 2 at Brisbane, Australia, where she and her passengers were given a warm reception. Following the call at Brisbane, the QE2 turned northward through the Great Barrier Reef to Indonesia and the Orient. The visits to China and Japan remain one of the key attractions of the great cruise. The QUEEN is regarded as a great tourist attraction in Japan, and many Japanese travel to see her when she arrives. The homeward leg of the cruise across the North Pacific is one of the single longest stretches of the cruise, but the great speed of the QUEEN turns it into a pleasurable break before the call in the Hawaiian Islands and the return to California. A West–East Panama Canal cruise brought the second transit of the waterway for the year and placed the QE2 in New York for the beginning of the 1983 transatlantic season.

The first arrival of the QE2 to New York in August 1982 virtually qualified as a second maiden arrival as New Yorkers celebrated the return of the largest ship to use the North River passenger ship terminal on a regular basis. The scene when she sailed was a little quieter. The QUEEN passes the twin towers of the Wrold Trade Center, which, at 1,250 feet, are only 25% taller than she is long.

In May 1983 Trafalgar House and the Cunard Line announced the completion of successful negotiations to purchase the fleet and goodwill of Norwegian American Cruises for $73 million. The two prizes gained were the magnificent five-star-plus passenger liners SAGAFJORD and VISTAFJORD, which enjoy reputations second to none, among the finest ships of their kind. Both liners were built to exacting standards and are designed to cater to the highest class of discerning world travelers. The quality of their staterooms, the superb design of their public rooms, and the gracious nature of their staff has earned for the SAGAFJORD and VISTAFJORD one of the highest percentages of repeat customers in the cruise industry. By this acquisition, Cunard was able to avoid the high costs of new constructions and at the same time increase their fleet with two ships that consistently received the "five star plus" rating given by the prestigious Fieldings Guide to Cruising. When Cunard wanted to expand, no finer acquisition was possible than Norwegian American Cruises, which instantaneously gave the QUEEN ELIZABETH 2 two medium-sized "sisters" with accommodations and reputations comparable to her own.

In May 1983 Trafalgar House, Cunard's parent company, also announced that they had acquired a 5% holding in the Peninsular and Orient Steamship Company. P & O operates a large fleet of passenger liners and other vessels and is the only other major British line engaged in the passenger business. The subsequent take-over bid received a lot of publicity and was eventually referred to the Monopolies Commission in Great Britain for evaluation. The commission ultimately decided in the spring of 1984 that it would not be against the public interest for the bid to proceed, and it now remains for Trafalgar House to make the next move.

Each fall the World's Premier Marathon Race takes place in New York City. October 23 was the race date in 1983, and some 17,000 runners from all 50 states and 68 foreign countries competed in the event. Among the vast throng of runners at the start of the Marathon were five members of the QE2's crew, who had been training on board and at various ports around the world whenever the opportunity arose.

The QUEEN was scheduled to dock in New York the morning of the marathon, but in order to be at the start on time, arrangements had to be made to collect the runners as the ship passed under the Verrazano Narrows Bridge. A launch came alongside the QE2 to collect the runners and then took them to Staten Island, where, after a quick BBC interview, the five were rushed by limousine to the assembly point for the start of the race. Those taking part were Grenville Cartledge, Brian Marshall, Mike Burgess, Barry Brennan, and Peter Burge, all of whom completed the course. Many of the QUEEN's crew members sponsored the New York Marathon runners, and as a result £1,778.11 p. ($2,700) was collected and shared between the National Lifeboat Institution and the Guide Dogs for the Blind Association. A guide dog has been christened Marathon and his picture can be seen on board the liner in one of the show cases.

The last closeup aerial study of the QUEEN ELIZABETH 2 done before the reconstruction of the aft deck area in December 1983. This view shows the ship in her pebble gray hull as she was from August 1982, after her return from the Falklands, until June 1983.

A rare juxtaposition of schedules finds the two largest liners in the world simultaneously anchored off St. Thomas in the fall of 1983. The QUEEN ELIZABETH 2, the largest liner in the world in terms of tonnage, arrives first and anchors, to be followed in by the Norwegian Caribbean liner NORWAY (ex-FRANCE, 1962), which swings around the stern of the Cunarder. The NORWAY, at 1,035 feet, is the longest passenger liner ever built.

The 67,703-ton QE2 and the 70,202-ton NORWAY ride at anchor in a magnificent Caribbean setting for the day before departing on their respective cruises. The QUEEN's schedule employs her in a series of Atlantic crossings and in cruises around the world, while the NORWAY normally operates from Miami on one-week cruises to St. Thomas and a Bahamian island. As the FRANCE, she was capable of 30-knot speeds like the QE2, but the re-engining as part of her transformation into the NORWAY cut her speed in half. Now only the QUEEN ELIZABETH 2 can make a 4½ day crossing of the North Atlantic as the fastest passenger liner in service.

The acquisition by Cunard of Norwegian American Cruises in 1983 brought two magnificent five-star-plus liners under Cunard management, the SAGAFJORD and VISTAFJORD. SAGAFJORD is shown here in April 1984 sporting her new Cunard funnel at Mazatalan, Mexico, while on a trans-Panama Canal cruise.

On November 28, 1983, the QUEEN ELIZABETH 2 arrived at Bremerhaven, West Germany, for her annual refit. The announcement that the work costing some £2½ million ($3,750,000) was being carried out in Germany generated a lot of adverse attention in the British press and the news was carried in many American papers. Very little attention was given to the fact that the major British shipyards had admitted they could not carry out the work on time, nor was much attention paid to the fact that Cunard already had spent £11 million on the ship in British yards since June 1982. A huge passenger liner cannot lie idle and wait for a berth to come along. She must receive the needed services promptly and be back on the line earning revenue as quickly as possible. At Bremerhaven the new Magradrome was fitted over the quarterdeck swimming pool, making it available in all weather. Powerful new launches also were fitted to assist in the transfer of passengers from ship to shore when required. Various sections of the ship were redecorated and refurbished in line with Cunard's ongoing program to maintain the QE2 as a vessel second to none.

In the eternal attempt to add variety to intineraries and cruise variations, a new twist will be the linking of world cruises on two great liners. A passenger may elect to go part way around the world on the QUEEN and then switch to the SAGAFJORD or VISTAFJORD at a convenient point. Thus one could have the best of both worlds in the grandure of the QUEEN ELIZABETH 2 and the intimacy of smaller vessels. The ability to tailor a vacation to particular desire or itinerary increases tremendously with the availability of two ships, and especially when combined with Concords flights to or from the ships.

The slate gray hull scheme was restored in June 1983, but the traditional Cunard Funnel was retained. The QUEEN is shown as she was from late June 1983 to late December 1983 when the Lido Deck was reconstructed at Bremerhaven.

Through April 15, 1984, the QUEEN ELIZABETH 2 had visited 145 different places around the world during her fifteen-year career. The most frequently visited port was New York, with 325 calls, and Southampton, the QUEEN's home port, was second with 240 dockings. In the future extensive use will be made of the Concorde supersonic transport to wisk passengers to and from the QE2 wherever she may be. In some years this, in fact, may amount to as many as 100 Concorde flights taking passengers to the QUEEN ELIZABETH 2, SAGAFJORD, and VISTAFJORD. The fly–cruise concept, therefore, reaches its ultimate combination with the Concorde and the QUEEN ELIZABETH 2.

What lies in the future for the QUEEN? A much longer and profitable career if all aspirations and plans reach fruition. Cunard is committed constantly to upgrading and improving the amenities of the liner in order to maintain a commitment to excellence. There is no reason why the vessel should not remain in service for another twenty years and steam profitably into the twenty-first century. Improvements in the nature and design of marine propulsion plants have moved ahead so dramatically in the past twenty years that a complete replacement of the existing system—which halved the fuel bill of the old QUEENS—by an even more economical one, is a definite possibility. Substantial savings in the QE2's fuel bill could prolong her useful career by an incalculable period, particularly if oil prices soar again. Some discussion periodically occurs about fuel-efficient, high-powered diesels capable of meeting even the 30-knot demands placed upon the QUEEN's

A great hotel requires constant attention if it is to maintain its reputation for excellence. The QE2 rarely remains the same for any long period of time. A recent major improvement involved the covering of the Lido Deck pool with a retractable Magrodome, making it into an all-weather facility and vastly expanding the amenities of the ship. The work was done at Bremerhaven, West Germany, and involved both extensive preparations and precision handling.

The after end of the Club Lido (ex-Q-4 Room) was sliced away as the QUEEN crossed the North Atlantic by workmen who had joined the ship for the voyage. Then, undergoing work to exacting specifications, the Lido Deck was prepared for the Magrodome, which was being finished at Bremerhaven.

machinery. Such discussions emphasize the fact that the QUEEN ELIZABETH 2 today could not be created for an investment of less than $300 million, and such a treasure requires constant vigilance and far-sighted concern to maintain in service.

The world belongs to the QE2, as much as the QUEEN to the world, since she is and remains unique. The 1984 great cruise was called "The Quintessential World Cruise." One of the highlights of this cruise occurred on February 29 at Kelang in Malaysia when at the invitation of His Royal Highness Sultan Salahuddin Abdul Aziz Shah of Selangor and Her Royal Highness The Tengku Ampuvan of Selangor, a banquet and entertainment in observance of the fourth annual QUEEN ELIZABETH 2 World Cruise Society was held for over 300 passengers at the Royal Palace. A fitting indication of the importance of the QUEEN to other countries and peoples was given by the message of His Royal Highness, in which he said:

> I am privileged and honoured to be given the opportunity to host this special function for the distinguished members of the World Cruise Society. Whilst it brings singular honour to me, it is equally an honour for all Malaysians and the State of Selangor in particular.
>
> On behalf of the people of Malaysia and the State of Selangor, I wish you all a warm welcome and I hope that your stay here will be a pleasant and memorable one. We sincerely hope that this magnificent ship will call

The huge Magrodome was slowly lifted from the yard by a powerful crane and positioned over the QE2's deck.

Once the positioning appeared exact, the Magrodome could be lowered onto the liner and welded in place. What had been one of the QUEEN's two outside pools and rarely usable on the North Atlantic was transformed into a universal asset.

135

At the Bremerhaven dry dock the QUEEN ELIZABETH 2's hull was thoroughly cleaned and painted as part of the annual refit. The 1080 feet of chain attached to each anchor is paid out on each side of the ship so that each anchor and all the links may be checked and painted. Note the bulbous bow to reduce water friction and the bow thruster doors on each side of the hull that are open for inspection. It is said that the QUEEN ELIZABETH 2's hull possesses the smooth, clean lines of a modern-day clipper ship.

The massive starboard propeller of the QUEEN dwarfs the workmen in the dry dock. Each of the six-bladed propellers has a weight of 31.75 tons and a diameter of 19 feet. Note also the careful arrangement of the keel blocks to support the massive weight of the liner when she is out of her element.

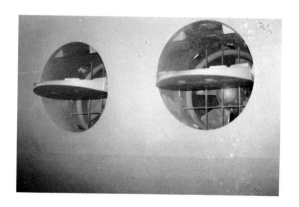

With the bow thruster doors open, it is possible to see the two variable-pitch propellers that are fitted into the tunnels running through the hull and which enhance the maneuverability of the QUEEN so much. Each propeller is 6.55 feet in diameter. The doors fit flush against the hull when the propellers are not in use.

at Port Kelang on all its round the world trips, so that many more people can enjoy our warmth and hospitality, and, that whilst this beautiful vessel makes our world smaller, we can in our journeys mutually help to bring peace, understanding and happiness.

The voyages of the QUEEN ELIZABETH 2 take her through many contrasts of cultures and civilizations. Every journey is different, and memorable, and important in one way or another to all those who sail on board her. The QUEEN is the last of the great luxury liners and when she goes, an era will end. While she remains, she is the most majestic and sophisticated passenger liner ever built and she bears testimony to the traditions that Cunard signifies: luxury, elegance, life enrichment, and international friendship.

The QUEEN ELIZABETH 2 steams into the Caribbean at the beginning of the 1984 World Cruise. The European, New York, and Florida passengers are on board for the trans-Canal section of the world cruise, which was totally sold out. The QUEEN is fresh from her annual overhaul and the installation of the new Magrodome and cruise launches at Bremerhaven.

CHAPTER EIGHT

Guide to the
Queen Elizabeth 2

The guide to the QE2, starting on the uppermost deck and working down and from forward to aft on each deck, describes the QE2 as she presently exists and the various changes that have been made since she first went into service in 1969. Some of the changes resulted in improvements in service and efficiency, but the majority were incorporated to upgrade the standard of passenger life on board. Other changes, such as those to accommodate the health spa and computer learning center, reflect the requirements of modern living.

THE MAST

Next to the funnel, the top of the mast is the highest part of the ship, being 169 feet, 1 inch above the waterline when the draft is 31 feet, 0 inch. Because the aerial for the satellite navigation system was situated at the top, the mast was 5 feet higher when the ship was commissioned. It was removed when the satellite receiver was updated. Unlike the old liners, the QE2 does not have a crow's nest in the mast, but there is access to the navigation lights and whistles from the inside. Part of the mast also acts as a duct to carry air up from the kitchens.

A more recent addition to the mast is the installation of a closed-circuit television camera that is directed toward the funnel. This enables the engineer officer on watch in the main control room to monitor the discharge from the funnel.

The mast of the QUEEN ELIZABETH 2 towers 200 feet, 1 inch above the keel of the liner, 169 feet, 1 inch above the waterline when the QUEEN is drawing her normal 31-foot draft. Next to the funnel, the top of the mast is the highest part of the ship.

The funnel of the QE2 dominates the silhouette of the liner. This view is an early one taken from the signal deck observation area and also shows the forward sports deck, all of which disappeared with the installation of the penthouse suites in 1972.

THE FUNNEL

From an external view, one of the most noticeable features of the QE2 is the funnel. With so much open deck space on the QE2, it is important that fumes and the occasional soot that is ejected from the funnel are carried well clear of the ship. To achieve this, used air from within the ship is ducted up behind the main boiler vents to create an area of high pressure and keep the exhaust up and away from the decks. In some wind conditions, however, this would not be sufficient, and the smoke would swirl back down again over the decks. To solve this, the shovel-shaped scoop was designed and introduced to direct a stream of air up and behind the vents. The design of the funnel was the result of many months of research carried out by Cunard's technical department and testing in the wind tunnel at the National Physical Laboratory at Teddington, Middlesex. The original black and white color scheme of the funnel was a break from Cunard tradition, but at the time it was felt that the red with black bands would not look appropriate with the modern functional design. In 1982 when the hull color was changed to a very light gray, the funnel was painted in Cunard colors and remained as such when the hull was changed again in 1983. The funnel, 204 feet, 1½ inches above the keel, is 5 feet higher than the mast.

SIGNAL DECK

The Signal Deck is the highest deck on the ship. Forward, the most important area is the bridge consisting of the wheelhouse and chart room. The bridge of the QE2 contains some of the most advanced as well as the more traditional navigational equipment used today. There are two Decca radars and a Raytheon Raycas collision avoidance system, Decca and Loran navigators and a Marconi direction finder for coastal position fixing, and a Magnavox Omega satellite navigator for ocean passages. Other equipment includes depth recorders, Doppler speed log, gyro and magnetic compasses, and automatic pilot for steering. Facilities are available for receiving weather reports from meteorological stations ashore.

The bridge is manned by at least one qualified officer 24 hours a day throughout the year. When she is at sea, there are always two officers on duty. In addition to his navigation duties, the officer on watch is responsible for the safety of the ship. In an emergency he can close the watertight doors from the bridge. He also has direct communication with the safety control room, the engine room, and the fire equipment lockers.

Astern of the mast is the upper level of the Penthouse Suites (described later) reached by a secluded elevator or stairway from either one of the two decks below. Across the open deck and near the base of the funnel are the pet kennels. They are reached from the inside by a stairway leading up from the starboard side of Boat Deck astern of the "D" stairway. There are accommodations for thirty-three animals. The kennels are staffed by graduates

The forward superstructure of the QUEEN ELIZABETH 2 appears massive when viewed from the bow of the ship. The bridge on signal deck sweeps across the ship from wing to wing, providing the officers on duty with a commanding view of the ship fore and aft. Beneath the bridge is the sports deck observation area, and beneath that the long line of windows indicate the officers' wardroom. The white boxlike shape in the center was added in 1972 and houses a portion of the kitchens. On either side of the quarterdeck forward are the QE2's cranes, capable of lifting 5 tons each, and forward of them on One Deck are the capstans and anchor chains.

The bridge is the center of navigation and safety for the QUEEN. The officers on duty can monitor the surrounding sea and communicate with any section of the ship instantaneously.

The radars, navigational equipment, bow thrusters, and watertight doors, to name only a few pieces of machinery, as well as all communications with the engine room can be operated from the bridge.

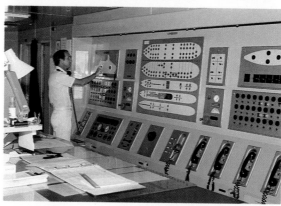

The engine room telegraph from the bridge to the engine room remains the official means of communication, even if continuous telephone contact is available. The system of lights clearly delineates what is needed at any time, with no possibility of error.

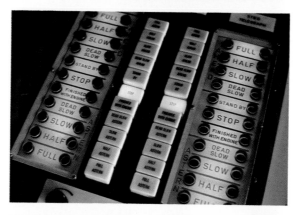

The QUEEN ELIZABETH 2 carries up-to-date charts of all the major, and many minor, coastlines and waterways of the world. This extensive library is continuously updated. The chart room is shown at the time of commissioning in 1969. (Photo courtesy of Brian Price.)

of England's Bellmead Kennel Maid Training School of Old Windsor. Dogs, the most frequent travelers, are more privileged than the rest—they even have their own lamppost.

SPORTS DECK

Reached from the stairs leading up from each side of the Boat Deck is the foremost observation area on the Signal Deck. The whole of the foredeck can be seen from this point. Immediately behind are the captain's and senior officers' quarters. Further aft is the lower level of the Penthouses. The Penthouse accommodations replaced an area of deck enclosed at the sides but open to the sky.

The Penthouses were added in two stages, the first at Southampton during the 1972 refit. The suites were prefabricated ashore and then lifted on board in two halves. Each of the rooms was given a distinctive atmosphere of its own. The then two premier units on each side forward are two-story, spanning Signal and Sports Deck, and connected by their own private internal stairway. The port-side accommodation was named the Trafalgar Suite and was designed and furnished as close as feasible to Lord Nelson's quarters on the H.M.S. VICTORY, even to the inclusion of a contemporary portrait of Lady Emma Hamilton. The starboard duplex, the Queen Anne Suite, was furnished to the style and period of the name it bears. Each of the luxury suites has two bathrooms and private verandahs overlooking the sea. The Queen Mary and Queen Elizabeth suites were added when the ship was having her annual overhaul at Bayonne, New Jersey, in 1977. These two split-level suites are more luxurious than any others available at sea and, in addition to verandahs, they have their own individual sundecks with panoramic views forward over the ocean.

The majority of the suite rooms were totally refurbished at Bremerhaven in December 1983. Some of them were fitted with whirlpool baths and had a personal videotape machine installed.

Next astern is the children's room, which was designed by Elizabeth Beloe and Tony Heaton while they were students of interior design at the Royal College of Arts. The room has retained its original design and includes a creche for the smallest children and a cinema with a sloping floor for older ones. Although inboard, the room is bright and gay with lots of colorful cupboards. Curvy fiber-glass screens divide part of the room, which makes it attractive for children playing games.

Further astern on each side of the deck are the radio and engineer officers' accommodations. The cabins are single berth and each has its own adjoining bathroom.

Doorways lead out onto the open deck—commonly referred to as the "helicopter deck." The large cross painted on the deck is a guide for helicopter pilots when making their approach.

The addition of the Penthouse Suites to the sports deck in 1972 and 1976 added a new dimension of luxury to travel on the QE2. The Penthouses are two decks high, with living room and bedroom facilities, as well as verandahs.

The radio room on the QUEEN ELIZABETH 2 frequently seems the busiest place on the ship, as communication is maintained with stations all over the world. A radio officer is on duty 24 hours a day.

BOAT DECK

Right forward on boat deck is the officers' wardroom and dining room, the windows of which look out over the foredeck. Outside the wardroom is the top of the "A" stairway. For those not put off by heights, there is an impressive view from the top all the way down to Five Deck. The radio room is situated on the port side of the square. This department is also manned 24 hours a day, with the officers in constant contact with the outside world by radio telegraphy, telex, or satellite communications.

Double glass doors lead from the square to the Queen's Grill Restaurant. When the ship was commissioned, this was known as the 736 Club, the number 736 being the one given by the ship's builders to identify the "job." The QE2 did not have a casino when first in service because of restrictive laws that existed in the United States. When the laws were relaxed, 736 was used as the casino for a brief period until one was permanently located on the upper deck.

At the time of the installation of the Penthouses, 736 was converted to the Queen's Grill. This area has enjoyed various decors over the years. The seashell sculpture provides a striking central focus to the room and complements the use of exquisite china, crystal, and tableware with the Queen of England's coat of arms on the bulkhead in the background.

Astern of the Queen's Grill is the Queen's Grill kitchen, which is totally dedicated to the 186 persons that can be accommodated in the restaurant.

Doors on the starboard side lead to the Queen's Grill Lounge. This room replaces the Coffee Shop and the Teenage Juke Box Room. Here coffee and light meals were available throughout the day and halfway through the night. The Juke Box Room had an area set aside for pinball machines, a juke box, and other teenage playthings, including distorting mirrors.

The QUEEN's Grill Restaurant was created in 1972 in place of the original 736 Club to accommodate the additional first-class passengers the QE2 could carry as a result of adding the Penthouses.

The port lifeboats of the QUEEN are seen in this 1972 view taken from the bridge wing in mid-Atlantic. The QE2 carries twenty lifeboats of various kinds and two large cruise tenders added in 1983. The foremost boat on each side is painted with a high-visibility orange and used for emergencies and rescues.

The boat Deck is used extensively by joggers. Five times around the U-shaped track equals 1 mile. Rounding the bend at the aft curve of the boat deck may mean you are nearly home. This view is in the Gulf of St. Lawrence during the 1983 Canadian cruise.

Part of the decor of the Queen's Grill is a magnificent polished wood plaque of the Royal Coat of Arms.

The "D" stairway on the boat deck gives entrance to the theater balcony, which can seat 136, or permits crossing the ship from the Queen's Grill Lounge to the video center and computer room, which occupy the old reading room since 1983.

The theater, designed by Gaby Schreiber, has a capacity for 627 patrons on two levels. The orchestra section is on the upper deck aft of the Tables of the World.

The Double Up–Double Down Room has been modified a number of times since 1969. The stage has been enlarged and acoustics improved since this 1972 view. The nightclub can seat over 800 and is one of the largest rooms ever created in a ship.

The curved staircase of the Double Down Room is one of its most spectacular features. The window area aft is now occupied by the camera shop.

The Queen's Grill Lounge has also enjoyed a variety of decors. In 1982 it was remodeled along with the Queen's Grill by Dennis Lennon, who was the original coordinating designer of the interior of the QE2.

Coming to the top of "D" stairway, the entrance can be seen to the cinema/theater balcony with seating for 136 people.

Further forward on the port side is the computer learning center, which was installed during the 1983 refit. The center features six IBM personal computers, videotape machines, and a library of educational films. This part of the ship was originally the London Gallery, where pictures were on display. When the Penthouses were installed, it was converted to a quiet reading room and housed interesting pictures depicting some of the old Cunard Line ships.

Astern on each side are suite rooms that take up the sites of the original shops. The QE2 probably has the largest selection of shops at sea. A full range of clothing is available in both the traditional and latest fashions. In addition to jewelry, cameras, perfume, souvenirs, books, and duty-free liquor, among other things, items indigenous to the countries the ship visits are made available. The shops were moved to the present location in 1972, this area having previously been a lounge with windows on either side and at the after end looking out over the boat deck. The interior design of the shops has changed periodically over the years, reflecting various vogues. An island bar originally was situated just astern of the center shop. The center shop was for a brief period known as the One Deck Shop, having been moved up from One Deck.

Doors on each side of the Hi Fi Shop lead out astern onto the open deck, which is referred to as the raised boat deck. A couple of steps down lead to the boat deck proper, and then, by walking right forward, you reach the steps leading to the sports deck forward observation area (situated under the wings of the bridge). The boat deck is popular with joggers and walkers—they must travel the U-shaped track five times to complete 1 mile.

All together there are twenty lifeboats of various types with a total capacity for 2,244 persons. (In addition, there are inflatable liferafts for 1,400 persons, which gives a total life-saving capacity for 25% more persons than the ship is certified to carry). Four of the larger boats have twin propellers, and they are used when the ship is at an anchorage port. The foremost boat on each side, painted high-visibility orange, is designed for use in emergencies.

The two new 45-foot cruise tenders that were installed on the ship in December 1983 were especially designed for improving the service at anchorage ports. They can carry 118 persons, and their 212-horsepower engines give a speed of 10 knots.

The casino on the QUEEN ELIZABETH 2 adds a new dimension to transatlantic travel and was made possible in the early 1970s by the removal of legal prohibitions. The casino has been modernized, enlarged, and improved a number of times.

UPPER DECK

A number of changes have taken place on this deck over the years. A major change was the demise of the Lookout Bar. In 1972 this was converted to a kitchen to serve the Tables of the World Restaurant. This restaurant was originally known as the Britannia Restaurant, and the total area was decorated throughout in the same manner. It is now divided into five different cultural-theme sections: Parisienne, Florentine, Londoner, Flaménco, and Oriental. Originally the center area housed escalators leading down to the Columbia kitchen to which the waiters had to go in order to obtain food orders. Although the removal of the popular Lookout Bar was disappointing, it nevertheless considerably improved the efficiency of service in the restaurant and increased the seating capacity to 792 persons.

At the starboard side entrance to the Tables of the World can be seen the Britannia figurehead. This was originally situated at the forward entrance to the restaurant by "A" stairway. The figurehead is carved out of Quebec yellow pine by Cornish sculptor Charles Moore and was presented to the ship by Lloyds of London.

As one moves astern on the starboard side one finds the entrance to the lower level of the theater/cinema, which has a capacity for 491 people. Gaby Schreiber, who was one of Britain's foremost woman designers, was responsible for the theater. It is also used as a conference room, and the captain holds a church service therein if the ship is at sea on a Sunday.

Next comes the Theater Bar on the starboard side. When crossing to the port side at "D" stairway, the Royal Standards can be seen, and between them is the commemorative plaque presented to the ship by Queen Elizabeth, the Queen Mother, on the occasion of the vessel's safe return from the South Atlantic. The plaque is a copy of the messages exchanged by signals made by the Queen Mother and the then master of the ship, Captain Peter Jackson.

Nearby is the cinema projection room and the control center for lighting and sound. Two large 70-millimeter projectors are used to show hundreds of films each year. On the world cruise alone enough films are carried to show a different one each day. Facilities also exist to show 16- and 35-millimeter films and audio slide presentations.

The Players Club Casino on the port side is the site of the old upper deck library. Forward is the Casino Hideaway Lounge and entrances to the cinema and restaurant.

Aft of the casino the photographers display pictures they took during the cruise. Passengers may also hand in their own films for processing on board by Ocean Pictures. The "E" elevator and red-carpeted stairway are nearby the display area. If anyone gets lost, this elevator is the place to go to, since it stops at every floor between the boat deck and Five Deck: a total of eight stops in all.

The shopping arcade on the boat deck aft occupies the two sides of the upper level of the principal transatlantic-class night-club, the Double Up Room. The shops are one of the busiest areas of the ship for passengers and provide a remarkable variety of curios and luxury items.

Just across to starboard is the cruise staff office, where a member of the staff is on duty to assist with leisure enquiries. Next door is the band's rehearsal room. The room and the office combined were originally the upper deck library.

Further astern is the Double Room. It was designed in its original form by Jon Bannenberg and was one of the largest rooms in the ship, covering 20,000 square feet and seating 800. Many functions are held here, such as cabaret and receptions. There is a large screen video projector in one corner. Passing through the Double Down Room on the port side there is the room known as the Double Down Suite. On the world cruise it is used by the social director for administrative and private functions. When the ship is on the transatlantic run, it is transformed into the Teenage Centre and houses popular video game machines and other activities. Next door is the tour office. During the world cruise American Express arranges and operates the shore excursions. Crossing over to the starboard side is the Flower Shop. The shop staff, in addition to supplying the floral requirements of passengers, also look after all the potted plants around the ship and the arrangements placed on the tables in the restaurants. Through the shop operators, George Davies & Son, and the Interflora organization passengers can arrange to have flowers sent worldwide in addition to receiving them on board from friends ashore.

Past the shop is the entrance to the Double Down Bar. This is a favorite spot for those who enjoy a piano bar atmosphere. Passing the table tennis area, one finds doors that lead out onto the open deck, where the paddle tennis court and golf practice nets and other deck games can be found. With the addition of the Magrodome in 1983, this area has been substantially altered. Steps lead up to the roof of the dome and then aft down to quarterdeck.

The Tables of the World Restaurant situated on the upper deck forward is the largest dining room on the QE2. Originally this facility was known as the Britannia Restaurant, but it was modernized and enlarged in 1972. The Oriental theme, one of five different decors, is shown in this view.

The Columbia Dining Room kitchens produce some of the finest cuisine anywhere on land or sea. Gleaming stainless steel surfaces await the rush of gourmet food preparation for some 600 passengers three times a day, seven days a week.

The great cauldrons in the Columbia kitchens can prepare 30 gallons of soup at a time. Recipes are created with hundreds of servings in mind rather than for an intimate dinner party. However, when the QUEEN is in the transatlantic service, passengers dining in the Columbia Restaurant may order any dish they please and it will be prepared for them personally, provided that the chefs are given adequate notice.

The Columbia Restaurant, with its floor-to-ceiling windows, offers a magnificent panorama of the sea for the diners. The modern pyramid lights on the tables glow softly as night approaches and provide a candle-lit atmosphere. The attention paid to individual passenger desires by the waiters in the Columbia is outstanding.

The centerpiece of the Columbia Restaurant is the silver vase given to Samuel Cunard by the citizens of Boston in July 1840. The captain and staff captain of the QUEEN ELIZABETH 2 sit at the captain's table on alternate nights in the Columbia and Tables of the World Restaurants. The celebrated "Midnight Buffet" of QE2 cruises usually is held in this room. (Photo courtesy of the Kathleen McDevitt Collection.)

QUARTERDECK

The hatch lid of the hold and the two associated cranes are on quarterdeck forward. Although not accessible to passengers, these can clearly be seen from the observation point on sports deck. Each crane has a safe working load of 5 tons, and they are used for loading vehicles and stores.

Inside and astern there is a very large area that houses the Columbia kitchen. The kitchen stretches the total width of the liner. A number of changes have taken place over the years that reflect the modernization of cooking appliances and ideas to improve hygiene and service efficiency. The Princess Grill is on the port side and is serviced by the Columbia kitchen. The Grill, maintained in its original design and color scheme of Bordeaux red velvet and leather, is often preferred by passengers who are assigned to the Queen's Grill. A striking visible feature is the life-sized statues by Janine Janet representing the four elements, fire, earth, air, and water, made entirely of marine items such as shells, coral, and mother-o'-pearl. The access to the Princess Grill is either by the "C" elevator or by spiral stairway up from One Deck.

Over 600 persons can be accommodated in the Columbia Restaurant. The captain has his table just to left of center. He also has a table in the TOW restaurant and alternates with the staff captain every other evening. The midnight buffet is usually held in the Columbia.

As one leaves the Columbia by the center entrance, there is a majestic panorama that stretches across the opposite wall. Three magnificent tapestries by Helena Barynina Hernmarck depict the launching ceremony of the liner by Her Majesty Queen Elizabeth II on September 27, 1967.

To the port side is the card room attractively designed in panels of green suede and baize, with a brighter green outlining the entrance to the two small booths raised up on one side. Past the "E" stairway and just forward of the Queen's Room is the library designed by Michael Inchbald. In addition to the continuously updated selection of magazines, novels, and reference books in English, there are foreign-language publications and large-type books. The library also houses a collection of videotapes for personal viewing.

On the starboard side of quarterdeck can be seen the toteboard, a traditional daily activity when the ship is at sea. Each morning the navigator on the bridge estimates the distance the ship will have steamed by noon for the previous 24 hours. Twenty consecutive figures are then marked on the tote board and passengers are invited to place a bet on the mileage they think the ship will have traveled. Shortly after midday the distance will be announced and winners can collect their share of the pool.

Nearby there is a large jigsaw puzzle placed on a table convenient to passengers strolling by: If you are lucky, you may see it completed during your trip or even finish it yourself. The Midships Bar is next, enjoying the same decor since the ship was launched, a credit to the designers, Dennis Lennon and Partners. At the after end of the room is a brass armillary sphere (showing the relationship of planets to the earth and the signs of the zodiac) that was presented to Cunard by the Institute of London Underwriters.

Spanning the width of the ship, the Queen's Room has a warm atmosphere day or night. It is the scene of many activities, from yoga classes in the morning, afternoon tea, and pre-dinner cocktail parties to the evening cabaret. The structural columns are encased in great inverted trumpets of white fiber-glass. The trumpet shape in reverse is reflected in the design of the white chairs upholstered in natural hide. At the forward end surrounded by the sculptured-appearing wall of walnut blocks and mirrors is the bronze bust of Her Royal Highness Queen Elizabeth II.

After leaving the Queen's Room, you come to the Club Lido. David Hicks designed the original room, which was known as the Q4. The QE2 herself was popularly known as the Q4 before she was christened. When a new ship was designed to follow the QUEEN MARY and the QUEEN ELIZABETH, it was referred to as the Q3. This plan was subsequently scrapped, and Q4 became the nickname for the QE2 when she first appeared on the drawing board. The first part of the major changes made to the Q4 came during the period it took

One of the most popular intimate bars on the QE2 is the Midships Bar on the starboard side of quarterdeck. Finished in dark-green suede, this room and its lounge provide an excellent meeting place before or after dinner in the Columbia.

Below right:
A pleasant place to relax is the Midships Bar lounge, with comfortable chairs and coffee tables overlooking the sea. Service is available during bar hours. Nearby is the jigsaw puzzle and the tote board.

The magnificent "D" stairway is shown upon leaving the Columbia Restaurant. The quarterdeck lobby features three superb tapestries created by Helena Barynina Hernmarck that depict scenes from the launching of the QUEEN ELIZABETH 2.

The Queen's Room is one of the largest rooms on the ship. (Photo courtesy of Brian Price.)

The quarterdeck library provides newspapers, magazines, and a large collection of books for the perusal and enjoyment of passengers. Some volumes on maritime subjects also may be purchased here.

The Q4 Room was designed by David Hicks as a late-evening nightclub and dance area for first class on the QUEEN ELIZABETH 2. Since 1983 this entire area has been completely rebuilt as the Club Lido.

The fitting of a prefabricated Magrodome over the Lido pool in 1983 added an enormous amount of useful space to the old Q4 Room and transformed the area into an all-weather Lido Club, complete with dance floor, bar, food serving area, pool, and comfortable lounging chairs.

The retractable Magrodome permits sunshine to bath the Lido pool when possible, and dancing under the stars in tropical settings.

the government to restore the ship to service after the 1982 Falklands campaign. The bar was removed from the after end and temporarily located on the port side. This enabled the after end to be opened up, thus creating a much lighter and therefore more versatile room in the daytime.

The second stage was carried out in 1983 in Bremerhaven. The bar was repositioned and the glass dome floor laid with adjacent bandstand and music and lighting control center. The prefabricated Magrodome was lifted into position within two days of the vessel's arrival at Bremerhaven. The retractable glass roof created a complete outdoor and indoor entertainment and leisure area.

ONE DECK

One Deck is the longest deck on the ship, having a total length from stem to stern of 963 feet. The forward part is known as the foredeck and, again, it can be seen from the observation point on the sports deck under the Bridge. When the ship is docking, an officer will be seen right forward supervising the mooring operations that take place from the deck below.

There are two anchors housed in the bow, each weighing 12½ tons. The anchor chain, or cable, as it is known to the seafarer, leads from the anchor up the hawse pipe and along the deck, passing round the capstan and then down into the chain locker. The total length of each chain is 1,080 feet, and the links are 4 inches in diameter and have a breaking strain of just over 500 tons. The anchor that can be seen on the port side of the foredeck is a spare. This used to be housed in the stem, but was repositioned following damage during a North Atlantic storm in 1981. During an earlier storm in 1976 the spare anchor was lost altogether and now lies on the ocean floor somewhere in the

The 963 feet of One Deck make it the longest deck in the ship. Far forward lies the foghorn, which can be heard for a distance of 10 miles. The huge anchor chains (1,080 feet long) and capstans also are here.

mid-Atlantic. Between the anchor the forward whistle can be seen mounted on the tripod. It is operated from the bridge. If the ship is in fog, it can be sounded automatically at regular intervals. Moving aft and inboard leads to the staff quarters. There are separate recreation rooms and dining areas with their own galleys for various crew members.

Just astern and in the passenger area is the photographers' darkroom. The team of five resident photographers will produce in the region of 1,600 pictures a day, in addition to making video films of the cruise.

Near "C" stairway on the port side is the Princess Grill Room Bar, which is a small room and now used only for private functions. A spiral stairway leads up to the Princess Grill.

On One Deck by the "D" stairway is the newly (1984) installed Harrod's of London shop. When the ship was commissioned, the One Deck Shop sold very exclusive jewelry. During the 1972 conversion the shop was moved up to the boat deck, and the area was converted into a bar known as the Club Atlantic. When the liner FRANCE ended her service on the North Atlantic run, staff members from the ship were employed on board the QE2 to work in the bar, and service was offered in five different languages. The bar was subsequently closed, and the area reverted to a shop specializing in china and crystal.

Before the installation of the Penthouses, the cabins on One Deck were the highest-grade accommodations available on the ship. Many of them have connecting doors to adjoining cabins. Over 70% of the cabins on board the QE2 are outboard, and all rooms have their own bath or shower. Each cabin also has a console for selecting music or radio news broadcasts from a selection of six channels, and there is a telephone connected to a central exchange from which calls can be made to anywhere in the world.

Toward the after end of One Deck by the "G" stairway the hair and beauty salon, operated by Steiner's of London, is found. Here, highly qualified hair stylists cater to men as well as women clients. The salon is constructed on the open plan principle, so that shampoo, setting, and drying areas are located in the main body of the room, with adjoining private sections for beauty care consultation and chiropodist treatment.

Doors lead out to the outside swimming pool and to the hamburger stand and bar nearby. At the after end of this area are facilities for skeet shooting.

TWO DECK

In the very foremost part of the vessel on Two Deck are the mooring winches. When the ship is in port, she will normally be made fast to the quay by three synthetic fiber ropes and three or four flexible steel wires at each end. The ropes are set up in position first, then followed by the wires. The wires have a breaking strain of 103 tons and are attached to self-tensioning winches that keep them tight irrespective of tidal conditions. Also in this area

The Princess Grill is the smallest of the four restaurants on the QUEEN ELIZABETH 2 and permits intimate dining in the height of luxury. The Princess Grill actually is located on the quarterdeck, but the graceful winding staircase leading to it starts on One Deck.

Few ships ever have offered to their passengers the amount of space the QUEEN ELIZABETH 2 can provide. The luxury and size of her first-class cabins on One Deck have rarely been equalled.

The Midships Lobby on Two Deck is the room most passengers see first when boarding the QUEEN ELIZABETH 2, since it was designed with the New York and Southampton terminals in mind. Boarding ramps connect directly to the Midships Lobby, where Cunard personnel are available to direct the 2,000 new passengers to their cabins.

155

The safety control room on Two Deck contains master diagrams of the ship showing all the safety control features. The SCR is manned 24 hours a day, 365 days of the year, and makes possible the most elaborate fire detection and prevention systems. The level of all fuel and water tanks is monitored in the SCR, which controls all pumping operations. (Photo courtesy of Brian Price.)

are the Bosun's stores and paint lockers, where enough stocks are carried to enable maintenance to be carried out on a continuous basis.

Near "B" stairway in the fore part of Two Deck is the finance office. Records are stored in a computer of the food, beverages, dry stores, and spare parts kept on board. Personal wage records of over 1,000 crew members are also held in the computers. The finance office is responsible for administering passenger personal accounts as well.

The Midships Lobby on Two Deck is the point where most passengers and visitors first come on board via the gangway that can be placed on either the port or the starboard side of the ship. This circular sunken area with green leather seating also makes an ideal meeting place.

On the starboard side near the gangway entrance is the suite used by the general manager of the QE2. Adjacent is the conference room utilized by the general manager and company staff. These two areas, which were installed in 1983, reflect corporate changes within the ship to render it a self-managing unit within the company.

Centrally placed within the ship, the safety control room (SCR) is, like the bridge and the engine room, manned 24 hours a day at sea and in port. Master plans of the ship showing all the safety features are on display.

The ship is divided into compartments, each of which can be made completely watertight by hydraulic doors remotely controlled from the bridge. Indicators set out in a diagram on the bridge and in the SCR show whether the doors are in the opened or the closed position.

The ship is also divided into eight zones with fire-resistant bulkheads and doors that can be remotely closed from the safety control room to prevent the fire from spreading. All the cabins and public rooms on the QE2 have automatic sprinklers installed. Should one of these be set off, an audible alarm is triggered in the SCR, and a visual indicator of the danger area will appear on the master diagrams. The break-glass alarm push buttons situated throughout the ship are similarly indicated. Certain areas are also equipped with smoke and vapor detectors that set off alarms in the SCR if any detaction is made. In addition, security petty officers specially trained in shipboard fire-fighting techniques patrol the ship at regular intervals to supplement the detecting aids. Every crew member joining the ship is required to undergo a QE2 safety familiarization course, and the certificate obtained upon completion must be revalidated at least every two years.

Consoles in the safety control room also indicate the amount of fuel, fresh water, and ballast water contained in all the tanks. Depending on the speed, fuel may be consumed at a rate of 20 to 25 tons per hour, so it is necessary to constantly adjust the water ballast tanks. The control of all pumping and transfer of water ballast and fuel is carried out from the control room. Accumulation of water in the bilges is sensed by electrically operated probes and indicated on another console where valves and pumps can be operated directly from the control room.

The bureau on Two Deck by the "F" stairway is the scene of many passenger-connected activities and can be compared with the reception desk at a large hotel. The staff on duty at the front desk can deal with the majority of passenger inquiries or channel them in the proper direction. On hand also are staff to deal with matters such as cabin allocations, baggage, and lost property. Nearby is the safe deposit box facility, which is administered by the bureau staff. Matters pertaining to passenger accounts are dealt with at the cashier's section of the bureau approached from the square at the "G" stairway. At the adjacent counter travel inquiries can be handled and future arrangements made. On both "F" and "G" squares there is a branch of Barclay's International Bank that offers a full range of banking and financial services, including foreign currency conversions, cashing travelers checks, and transfers of funds. All major credit cards are accepted.

The doctor's consultation room and waiting lounge are located on the port side of "G" square. A doctor is in attendance at regularly posted hours during the day, at which time passengers may visit without having made a prior appointment.

During the world cruise an office is set up on the starboard side of "G" square. Known as the manifest office and manned by a staff of five and with the assistance of computers, this office handles all passports, visas, and immigration matters. At the extreme after end of Two Deck are the mooring arrangements similar to those described at the forward end of the vessel.

THREE DECK

An impressive indication of the length and structure of the ship can be seen on Three Deck. As one looks aft from the forward end, the deck head appears to come into contact with the deck owing to the curvature built into the construction of the ship. The synagogue designed by Professor Misha Black is located by the "A" stairway. The room is peacefully decorated in blue with ash panels.

Hidden away on Three Deck is the room that houses the main sound reproduction console. Also included is a small studio for live broadcasts.

Further aft is the telephone exchange. Staff are on duty at the exchange day and night, as all calls made from passenger cabin telephones must be connected through the exchange operators. An automatic exchange handles calls made from staff quarters and operational areas of the ship. Overseas calls, whether by radio or via satellite, are channeled through the exchange. At the after end of Three Deck on the starboard side is a launderette and ironing area for passengers' personal use.

FOUR DECK

Four Deck is almost entirely taken up with passenger cabins and with crew quarters at the extreme ends fore and aft. Gangways are sometimes located on Four Deck, and facilities exist for cars to be taken on through the same entrances.

The Three Deck corridor provides an impressive indication of the length of the QUEEN ELIZABETH 2. As one looks aft from the forward end, the ceiling appears to come into contact with the floor, to use land terminology, because of the length and curvature of the ship.

FIVE DECK

As with Four Deck, there is crew accommodation at the extreme ends of Five Deck, with passenger cabins in between. Along each side of the ship there are nine shell doors. These doors form part of the hull and are very strongly constructed. When closed, they are secured by steel bolts and are watertight. The doors have various uses such as for gangways, stores, and cars. When the ship is at anchor, pontoons are lowered down from the boat deck and are made fast by the opening in use, which provides boarding platforms for the ship's launches. Amidships on each side, the doors give access to the bunkering stations. Oil can be taken on board at a rate of 600 tons per hour on each side. Water can also be taken aboard at the same place.

Watertight doors are fitted at regular intervals all the way along each side of Five Deck and below. The doors divide the ship into fifteen separate watertight compartments and are tested every day the ship is at sea.

SIX DECK

Six Deck is very much a working area of the ship, and the passageway that runs from forward to aft on the starboard side is known as the "working alleyway." Crew quarters stretch from the forward and down the port side to the after end. There is a fully staffed launderette for crew use near the "A" stairway, and further aft is an administrative office that deals with day-to-day affairs of the crew members.

Next is the Printer's Shop. A variety of items are produced here, ranging from menus, daily programs, newspapers, and special invitations to general stationery requirements.

The hospital is located by the "C" stairway on Six Deck. Being near the waterline and at the center of the ship, it is free from movement that is sometimes evident in higher parts of the ship. Its location adjacent to working areas also makes it easily accessible to the crew. Consisting of four multibed wards and one single-bed ward, the hospital contains a total of thirteen beds. The single-bed ward is used mostly as either an intensive care unit or in situations where isolation is required. Serving the wards is a duty room, where indicators show if a patient requires attention. There is also an oxygen and nitrous oxide storage room from which direct lines of each gas lead to every bed in the wards, operating theater, and dental surgery. A well-stocked pharmacy caters to a wide variety of medical complaints. To assist with diagnoses there is a small laboratory where pathological tests can be carried out.

Should surgery be required, there is a fully equipped operating theater. Basic operating instrument packs are kept ready and are resterilized at regular intervals. Specialized instruments can be quickly sterilized in the autoclave.

Separate but enclosed within the hospital area are a physiotherapy ward, a lead-lined x-ray room, a fully equipped dental surgery, and a specially refrigerated compartment should death suddenly occur.

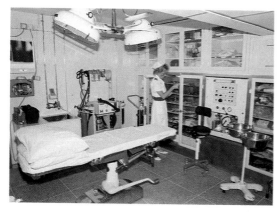

The fully equipped hospital is located by the "C" stairway on Six Deck, where it will be most stable. It is possible for the two doctors and three nurses to perform almost any operation if the situation is critical.

158

The hospital is manned by two doctors, three nursing sisters, and three medical attendants. During the annual world cruise this team is supplemented with a fourth nursing sister, a physiotherapist, and a dentist. Clinics are held twice daily for both the passengers and the crew. Should an unexpected emergency occur outside clinic hours, the whole medical team can be called by a special alert procedure to attend a patient whatever their location. The team and accompanying emergency equipment can be assembled within a very few minutes.

Moving toward midships, there are the electrical and plumbers workshops and the technical offices by the entrance to the engine room.

Aft of the engine room is the Golden Door Spa at Sea. Access is from Five Deck via the "F" stairway or elevator. The spa, the first ever at sea, was introduced in 1982 and is directed by the Golden Door of Encino, California. A total fitness and exercise program is run by Golden Door personnel to fulfill the needs of individual passengers. Daily activities include yoga, aerobic exercises, jogging, swimming, and lectures on nutrition, stress management, and a variety of other topics relating to health. The spa has a large exercise area, a pool with a teak platform for hydrocalisthenics, and three large Jacuzzi whirlpool baths. The latter facilities replace the Turkish baths.

SEVEN AND EIGHT DECKS

Right forward on Seven and Eight Decks there is the bulk beer stores holding a total of 13,000 gallons in twenty-seven tanks. The tanks are in an air-conditioned room from where the beer is piped directly to the bars.

The domestic storerooms are all situated forward in the ship and provide a total capacity of about 20,000 cubic feet of storage. Additional space is gained by using the holds when the ship is on the annual world cruise. Hold No. 2 is used exclusively for the storage of wines and spirits. The retail value of the stock of spirits alone at the start of the world cruise is in excess of $2 million. Over 20,000 bottles of wine are carried, varying in price from $7.50 to $440 a bottle.

Cars driven on board at Four or Five Deck level are taken below to the holds by the two car lifts. The lifts are of the turret type, so they can turn, thus enabling the cars to be driven off into the holds in any direction.

On Seven Deck, reached from the "C" stairway or elevator, is the second indoor swimming pool, saunas, and gymnasium. This area was completely refurbished in 1984.

THE ENGINE ROOM AND ASSOCIATED MACHINERY

The main control room is the senior watchkeeping station in the machinery spaces and is located on a flat above the main alternator room. It is air-conditioned and sound-proofed. Windows look out over the turbo-alternator machinery. On the forward end is the switchboards and group starter panels

Those who relish a good piece of meat can have an abundance of prime beef, lamb, pork, and poultry of all kinds on the QUEEN ELIZABETH 2, where the cold-storage rooms are stocked to overflowing at the start of every voyage.

The main turbine control room is located above the main alternator room and is air-conditioned and sound-proofed. The workings of the engine room can be monitored both through the maze of gauges and through the windows. (Photo courtesy of Brian Price.)

159

The QUEEN ELIZABETH 2 was supplied with fifty-eight watertight doors by Stone Manganese Marine Limited. The doors can be closed automatically from the bridge, or manually, as shown in this picture. (Photo courtesy of the Frank O. Braynard Collection.)

for main and auxilliary machinery. The main control console houses electrical controls for the main alternator run-up schemes and various electrical circuit switching, main boiler control systems, including combustion control, main engine telegraphs, feed systems and forced draft fan controls, domestic service systems, stabilizer, and bow thruster controls. There is a comprehensive telephone and public address system, from which, as in the turbine control room, the officer has direct communications with all machinery spaces.

The turbine control room is located in the engine room forward of the main turbines and has similar features to the MCR. The turbines are remotely controlled from this room and it replaces the traditional engine maneuvering platform. All remote controls and gauges associated with the complete control of the main power plant are located in this area.

The original thinking that went into the machinery design dates back to 1954 when John Brown (Clydebank) were asked to prepare proposals and designs for a new ship, at that time known as the Q3, to replace the old QUEENS. When the order was placed for the QE2, the machinery was largely based on that proposed for the larger quadruple-screw ship.

Schedule requirements for a weekly transatlantic service call for an average speed of 28.5 knots, which necessitated a service shaft horsepower of between 85,000–95,000. In order to give a reserve of power, the main turbines were designed for a maximum output of 110,000 horsepower.

The power is shared equally between the two propellers, each driven by an independent set of turbines. Each unit is comprised of a high-pressure and a double-flow low-pressure turbine that transmit their power through dual tandem reduction gears. Two sets of double reduction geared turbines are supplied with steam from three high-pressure water tube boilers.

Designed by Foster-Wheeler and manufactured by John Brown Engineering, the boilers were the largest ever to be fitted in a marine installation. Each boiler weighs 278 tons and is fitted with superheaters designed to operate at outlet temperatures of 1,000 degrees Fahrenheit and 850 pounds per square inch of pressure.

The propellers are attached to the 250-foot-long shafts by large nuts with an internal diameter of 23 inches, which at the time were the largest ever made. The two six-bladed propellers were supplied by Stone Manganese Marine, Ltd., at a cost of over £500,000. Each weighs 31.75 tons and has a diameter of 19 feet and a pitch of 21.65.

Electricity is supplied by three AEI turbine generators, each of which is capable of producing 5,500 kilowatts of power at 3,300 volts, 60 hertz, and at the time were the largest ever to be built for shipboard use.

The two bow thruster units, one of which is 4 feet to the rear of the other, were supplied by Stone Manganese Marine, Ltd., London. Both are contained in separate tunnels and pass laterally through the hull. Each unit has two variable-pitch blades 6.55 feet in diameter driven by an AEI 1000 low-

The engine room of the QUEEN contains many pieces of auxiliary machinery such as circulating pumps for the cooling system employing sea water, turbo-alternators (to the left) and, a vital consideration for tropical cruises, an air-conditioning plant (to the right). (Photo courtesy of Martin S. Harrison, Second Engineer Officer.)

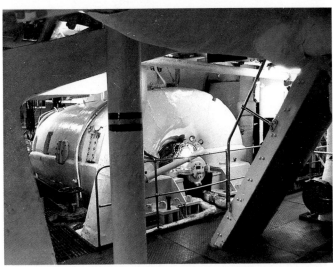

The QUEEN ELIZABETH 2 has two high-pressure and two low-pressure turbines to supply the power to turn the two propeller shafts. The starboard engine low-pressure turbine is shown here within its normal casing. (Photo courtesy of Martin S. Harrison, Second Engineer Officer.)

An extraordinary maze of steel blades is revealed when the starboard engine low-pressure turbine is opened up for its quadrennial survey during one of the ship's annual refits. (Photo courtesy of Martin S. Harrison, Second Engineer Officer.)

The ship's three 5.5-megawatt turbine-driven alternators supply the entire electrical requirements of the liner and could meet the needs of a city of 10,000–20,000 inhabitants. (Photo courtesy of Martin S. Harrison, Second Engineer Officer.)

The view across the engine room from above the port engine gear box toward the starboard engine. The engine room had been recently repainted when these photographs were taken. (Photo courtesy of Martin S. Harrison, Second Engineer Officer.)

The propeller shafts of the QUEEN ELIZABETH 2 are 250 feet long and approximately 23 inches in diameter. In general terms, they transfer the power from the machinery in the engine room to the 31.75-ton propellers outside the hull that push the ship. (Photo courtesy of Martin S. Harrison, Second Engineer Officer.)

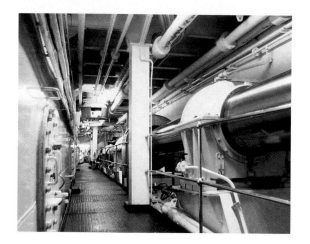

pressure electric motor controlled directly from the bridge. Flush-mounted hydraulically operated tunnel doors preserve the streamlining of the hull when the thrusters are not in use.

The semibalanced rudder, which weighs 75 tons, was manufactured in Norway by the firm of A/S Strommens Vaerksted. It is controlled by a four-ram electrohydraulic steering gear supplied by Brown Brothers of Edinburgh. Although one is sufficient, it has two pumping units. Under normal conditions the steering gear is automatically operated from the bridge, but in an emergency the rudder can be controlled from a position local to the machinery.

The Denny-Brown AEG stabilizers were manufactured by Brown Brothers. Each of the four retractable fins has an area of 70 square feet. When not in use, the fins are hinged forward into recesses in the ship's hull. All four fins are controlled from a central point, but are hydraulically independent of each other and are fully automatic in action.

The QE2 represents one of the most complex integrations of design and machinery ever attempted by man—a vessel capable of going almost anywhere on the globe covered by oceans, seas, and rivers with nearly 2,000 passengers and 1,000 crew at a speed in excess of 30 miles an hour in the height of luxury. When she went into service in 1969, she was revolutionary in many ways. Today, at mid-point in her career she still remains ultramodern, and continued efforts will be made to keep her so.

The two bow thrusters located toward the bow in tunnels transversing the ship are controlled from the bridge. By forcing water through the tunnels, they can swing the QUEEN *in either direction and, in fact, make it possible for her to turn completely around in a circle little more than her length.*

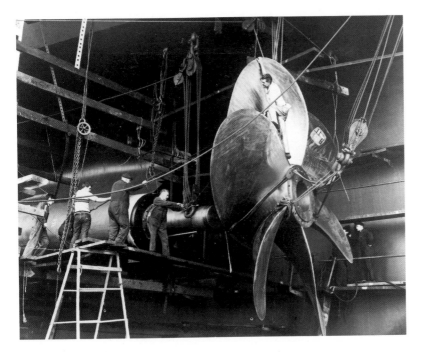

The QUEEN ELIZABETH 2 *is the largest twin-propellered passenger liner ever built. The old* QUEENS *had four. The propellers each weigh 31.75 tons, have six blades, and are 19 feet in diameter, with a pitch of 21.65 feet. The propeller is shown during installation at John Brown & Sons Ltd., Clydebank, Scotland (1967). (Photo courtesy of the Frank O. Braynard Collection.)*

163

APPENDIX ONE

S.S. Queen Elizabeth 2

Builders: Upper Clyde Shipbuilders
Keel laid: 5 July 1965
Launched: 20 September 1967
Maiden voyage: 2 May 1969
Port of registry: Southampton
Signal letters: GBTT
Official number: 336703

TONNAGE

Gross tonnage: 67,139.94
Net tonnage: 37,218.08

DIMENSIONS

Length overall: 963 feet, 0 inch (293.5 m)
Breadth overall: 105 feet, 2 and one-half inches (32.0 m)
Bridge height of eye: 95 feet, 0 inch (29.0 m)
Bridge to stem: 238 feet, 2 inches (72.6 m)
Bridge to stern: 724 feet, 10 inches (220.9 m)
Mast height above keel: 200 feet, 1 and one-half inches (61.0 m)
Funnel height above keel: 204 feet, 1 and one-half inches (62.2 m)

DRAFT

Light draft: 24 feet, 4 and one-half inches (7,429 mm)
freeboard: 31 feet, 9 and one-quarter inches (9,864 mm)
displacement: 33,365 tons
tons per inch: 147
Freshwater immersion allowance: 7 and one-half inches (190 mm)

Loaded draft: 32 feet, 7 and one-half inches (9,944 mm)
freeboard: 23 feet, 6 and one-quarter inches (7,169 mm)
displacement: 48,886 tons
tons per inch: 164.6
Dead weight: 15,521 tons

MACHINERY

Engine builders: John Brown Engineering
Engine: Steam turbine double reduction
Boilers: 3 Foster-Wheeler
Registered horsepower: 55,000 per shaft
Propellers: 2 six bladed; diameter, 19.0 feet; pitch, 21.65 feet
Bow thrusters: 2 Stone Kamewa; 1000 horsepower per unit; 6.65-foot variable-pitch propeller
Stabilizers: 4 Deny Brown
Steering gear: Brown Bros. 4 ram electrohydraulic

TANKS

Fresh water: 1,156 tons
Laundry: 1,768 tons
Fuel: 6,425 tons
Reserve feed: 1,277 tons
Ballast: 3,724 tons

ANCHORS

Forward: 3 at 12 and one-half tons
cables: 2 at 4 inches by 12 inches shackles
Aft: 1 at 7 and one-quarter tons
cable: 1 at 3 inches by 8 inches shackles

PASSENGER AND SAFETY CERTIFICATES

Passengers: 1,900
Crew: 1,015
Total: 2,915

Lifeboats: 20, total capacity 2,244
Life rafts: 56, total capacity 1,400
Buoyant apparatus: 5, total capacity 100
Life jackets: adult: 3,527
                    children: 145
                    Total: 3,672

APPENDIX TWO

*Ports Visited by the
Queen Elizabeth 2 and
Date of Maiden Arrival*

22 Mar 1975	Acapulco, Mexico
1 Oct 1983	Ajaccio, Corsica
28 May 1981	Alesund, Norway
7 Apr 1976	Alexandria, Egypt
25 Jul 1974	Andalsnes, Norway
27 Dec 1973	Antigua, Leeward Islands
8 Feb 1971	Aruba, Netherlands Antilles
20 May 1982	Ascension Island, South Pacific (rendezvous only)
21 Apr 1973	Ashdod, Israel
4 Feb 1978	Auckland, New Zealand
25 Mar 1975	Balboa, Panama
22 Feb 1975	Bali, Java
22 Nov 1969	Barbados, Windward Islands
29 Apr 1974	Barcelona, Spain,
23 Jul 1981	Bar Harbor, United States
13 Feb 1978	Bay of Islands, New Zealand
29 Jul 1973	Bergen, Norway
25 Mar 1971	Bermuda, North Atlantic
11 Feb 1975	Bombay, India
25 Dec 1981	Bonaire, Netherlands Antilles
1 Oct 1971	Boston, United States
9 May 1975	Bremerhaven, Germany
24 Feb 1983	Brisbane, Australia
30 Apr 1974	Cannes, France
11 Oct 1973	Canso Strait, Nova Scotia
10 Nov 1970	Cape Town, South Africa
26 Mar 1975	Cartagena, Columbia
15 Nov 1969	Cherbourg, France
27 May 1969	Cóbh, Irish Republic
17 Feb 1975	Colombo, Sri Lanka
9 Oct 1973	Come by Chance, Newfoundland
17 Mar 1980	Constanta, Rumania
19 Jul 1972	Copenhagen, Denmark
12 Aug 1983	Corner Brook, Newfoundland
25 Mar 1975	Cristobál, Panama
3 Dec 1969	Curaçao, Netherlands Antilles
30 Oct 1970	Dakar, Senegal
10 Mar 1979	Darien, People's Republic of China
5 Mar 1980	Djibouti, French Territory of Afars and Issas
7 Nov 1970	Durban, South Africa

6 Sep 1982	Falmouth, England
3 Jul 1981	Flaam, Norway
1 Feb 1971	Freeport, Bahamas
18 May 1982	Freetown, Sierra Leone
28 Jul 1973	Geiranger, Norway
21 May 1983	Genoa, Italy
24 Apr 1970	Gibraltar, Crown Colony
23 Nov 1969	Grenada, Windward Islands
27 May 1983	Grytviken, South Georgia
24 Apr 1973	Haifa, Israel
11 Oct 1973	Halifax, Nova Scotia
21 Jul 1972	Hamburg, Germany
25 Jul 1973	Hammerfest, Norway
13 Jul 1979	Hellesylt, Norway
20 Feb 1978	Hobart, Tasmania
27 Feb 1975	Hong Kong, Crown Colony
15 Mar 1975	Honolulu, Hawaii
29 Sep 1983	Ibiza, Balearic Islands
29 Apr 1970	Istanbul, Turkey
13 Mar 1979	Kagoshima, Japan
29 Mar 1983	Kailua Kona, Hawaii
15 Feb 1984	Keelung, Taiwan
8 Jan 1970	Kingston, Jamaica
5 Mar 1975	Kobe, Japan
1 Mar 1977	Kota Kinabalu, Borneo
11 Jan 1971	La Guaira, Venezuela
20 Mar 1982	Lahaina, Hawaii
16 Apr 1982	Lanzarote, Canary Islands
25 Apr 1969	Las Palmas, Canary Islands
2 May 1969	Le Havre, France
28 Apr 1969	Lisbon, Portugal
19 Mar 1975	Los Angeles, United States
3 Nov 1970	Luanda, Angola
2 Apr 1970	Madeira, North Atlantic
18 Feb 1982	Madras, India
8 Feb 1975	Mahe, Seychelles
12 Oct 1982	Malaga, Spain
11 Mar 1978	Manilla, Philippines
24 Nov 1969	Martinique, Windward Islands
4 Apr 1978	Mazatlán, Mexico
12 Feb 1982	Mauritius, Indian Ocean
22 Feb 1978	Melbourne, Australia
6 Jun 1973	Messina, Sicily

18 Feb 1978   Milford Sound, New Zealand
5 Feb 1975   Mombasa, Kenya
4 Feb 1979   Montevideo, Uruguay
9 Feb 1983   Moorea, Society Islands

10 Mar 1977   Nagasaki, Japan
2 May 1970   Naples, Italy
10 Mar 1971   Nassau, Bahamas
2 Oct 1982   Newport, United States
7 May 1969   New York, United States
15 Jan 1972   Norfolk, United States

12 Apr 1976   Odessa, Russia
18 Jul 1972   Oslo, Norway

3 Oct 1983   Palermo, Sicily
30 Apr 1972   Palma, Balearic Islands
28 Feb 1982   Pattaya, Thailand
1 Mar 1984   Penang, Malaya
25 Apr 1982   Philadelphia, United States
27 Apr 1970   Piraeus, Greece
30 Dec 1970   Port au Prince, Haiti
8 Dec 1980   Port Canaveral,
              United States
21 Dec 1971   Port Everglades,
              United States
23 Feb 1982   Port Kelang, Malaya
1 Mar 1978   Port Moresby, Papua
29 Dec 1969   Port of Spain, Trinidad
8 Mar 1980   Port Said, Egypt
7 Mar 1980   Port Suez, Egypt
10 Mar 1982   Pusan, South Korea

20 Jul 1981   Quebec, Canada
19 Mar 1983   Quing Dao,
              People's Republic of China

11 Feb 1983   Rarotonga, Cook Islands
17 Nov 1970   Rio de Janeiro, Brazil
4 Dec 1974   Rotterdam, Holland

10 Feb 1971   St. Croix, Virgin Islands
13 Dec 1982   St. Kitts, Leeward Islands
17 Dec 1970   St. Lucia, Windward Islands
17 Nov 1971   St. Maarten, Leeward Islands
25 Nov 1969   St. Thomas, Virgin Islands
24 Jan 1971   St. Vincent, Windward Islands
20 Nov 1970   Salvador, Brazil
1 Apr 1978   San Francisco, United States

2 Apr 1973   San Juan, Puerto Rico
10 Feb 1976   Santo Domingo,
              Dominican Republic
20 Feb 1975   Singapore, Malaysia
25 Jul 1973   Skarsvaag, Norway
        1969   Southampton, England
30 May 1980   Stavanger, Norway
11 Feb 1978   Suva, Fiji
24 Feb 1978   Sydney, Australia
26 Jun 1979   Sydney, Nova Scotia

5 Feb 1978   Tahiti, Society Islands
16 May 1973   Tangier, Morocco
26 Apr 1969   Tenerife, Canary Islands
11 Feb 1981   Tongatapu, Tonga Islands
10 Nov 1979   Tortola, Virgin Islands
8 Feb 1979   Tristan de Cunha,
              South Atlantic Ocean
7 Jul 1981   Tromso, Norway
27 Jul 1973   Trondeim, Norway

9 Feb 1978   Vava'u, Tonga Islands
12 Jun 1974   Vigo, Spain
3 Jul 1981   Vik, Norway

16 Feb 1978   Wellington, New Zealand

16 Mar 1980   Yalta, Russia
7 Mar 1975   Yokohama, Japan

APPENDIX THREE

Cunard Line

Master Mariners

Who Have Sailed in

Command of the QE2

23 Dec 1968   Captain William E. Warwick, C.B.E., R.D., R.N.R.

12 Jun 1969   Captain George E. Smith

17 Oct 1969   Captain F. J. Storey, R.D., R.N.R.

8 May 1970   Captain J. E. Woolfenden, R.D., R.N.R.

19 Jun 1970   Captain William J. Law, R.D., R.N.R.

3 Jun 1971   Captain Mortimer Hehir

6 Aug 1973   Captain Peter Jackson

22 May 1976   Captain R. H. Arnott, R.D., R.N.R.

13 Apr 1977   Captain Lawrence R. W. Portet, R.D., R.N.R.

26 Aug 1978   Captain T. D. Ridley, R.D., R.N.R.

13 Mar 1982   Captain A. J. Hutcheson, R.D., R.N.R.

15 May 1983   Captain Robin Wadsworth

9 Apr 1984   Captain Keith H. Stanley

BIBLIOGRAPHY

Albion, Robert Greenhalgh,
  *Naval and Maritime History, An
  Annotated Bibliography*, 3rd ed.,
  Connecticut, 1963.

Anderson, Roy,
  White Star, Lancashire, 1964.

Angas, Commander W. Mack,
  Rivalry on the Atlantic, 1833–1939, New
  York, 1939.

Appleyard, Rollo,
  Charles Parsons: His Life and Work,
  London, 1933.

Armstrong, Warren,
  Atlantic Highway, New York, 1962.

Arnott, Captain Robert H.,
  Captain of the Queen, Kent, 1982.

Aylmer, Gerald,
  R.M.S. MAURETANIA: *The Ship and Her
  Record*, London, 1934.

Beaudean, Baron Raoul de,
  Captain of the Ile, translated by Salvator
  Attanasio, New York, 1960.

Beesley, Lawrence,
  The Loss of the S.S. TITANIC, Boston,
  1912.

Bensted, C.R.,
  Atlantic Ferry, London, 1936.

Bisset, Sir James,
  Ship Ahoy!, Liverpool, 1932.

——, *Sail Ho*, London, 1958.

——, *Tramps and Ladies*, London, 1959.

——, *Commodore*, London, 1961.

Bonsor, N. R. P.,
  North Atlantic Seaway, 2nd ed., in five
  volumes, Jersey, Channel Islands, 1980.

——, *South Atlantic Seaway*, Jersey,
  Channel Islands, 1983.

Bowen, Frank C.,
  A Century of Atlantic Travel, 1830–1930.
  Boston, 1930.

Brady, Edward Michael,
  Marine Salvage Operations, New York,
  1960.

Braynard, Frank O.,
  By Their Works Ye Shall Know Them,
  New York, 1968.

Brinnin, John Malcolm,
  The Sway of the Grand Saloon, New
  York, 1971.

Broackes, Nigel,
  A Growing Concern, London, 1979.

Corson, F. Reid,
  *The Atlantic Ferry in the Twentieth
  Century*, London, 1930.

Cunard Line,
  *The Cunarders 1840–1969, A
  Transatlantic Story Spanning 129 Years*,
  Cunard Line: London, 1969.

Dunn, Laurence,
  North Atlantic Liners, 1899–1913,
  London, 1961.

Dunnett, Alastair M.,
  The Donaldson Line, 1854–1954,
  Glasgow, 1960.

Fry, Henry,
  *The History of North Atlantic Steam
  Navigation*, London, 1896.

Gibbs, C. R. Vernon,
  Passenger Liners of the Western Ocean,
  London, 1957.

——, *British Passenger Liners of the Five
  Oceans*, London, 1963.

Grattidge, Harvey,
  Captain of the Queens, New York, 1956.

Hoehling, Adolph and Mary,
  The Last Voyage of the LUSITANIA, New
  York, 1956.

Hyde, Francis E.,
  *Cunard and the North Atlantic,
  1840–1973*, London, 1975.

Isherwood, J. H.,
 Steamers of the Past, Liverpool, 1966;
 also the monthly drawings and
 descriptions in *SEA BREEZES*.

Kludas, Arnold,
 Great Passenger Ships of the World, five
 volumes, Cambridge, 1975.

Lauriat, Charles E.,
 The LUSITANIA's Last Voyage, Boston and
 New York, 1915.

Lee, Charles E.,
 The Blue Riband, London, 1930.

Lindsay, W. S.,
 History of Merchant Shipping, London,
 1876.

Lord, Walter,
 A Night to Remember, New York, 1955.

Maber, John,
 North Star to Southern Cross, Lancashire,
 1967.

McLennan, R. S.,
 Anchor Line 1856–1956 Glasgow, 1956.

Maginnis, A. J.,
 The Atlantic Ferry, London, 1900.

Maxtone-Graham, John,
 The Only Way to Cross, New York,
 1972.

Moody, Bert,
 Ocean Ships, London, 1971.

Oldham, Wilton J.,
 The Ismay Line, Liverpool, 1961.

Potter, Neil,
 The MARY, London, 1961.

—— and Jack Frost, *The ELIZABETH*,
 London, 1965.

——, *The QUEEN ELIZABETH 2*, London,
 1969.

Preble, Rear-Admiral G. H.,
 History of Steam Navigation,
 Philadelphia, 1883.

Shaum, John H., Jr., and
 William H. Flayhart III,
 Majesty at Sea, The Four Stackers,
 Cambridge, 1981; New York, 1981.

Smallpeice, Sir Basil,
 Of Comets and Queens, Shrewsbury,
 1981.

Smith, Eugene W.,
 *Passenger Ships of the World—Past and
 Present*, Boston, 1963.

Spedding, Charles T.,
 Reminiscences of TransAtlantic Travelers,
 Philadelphia, 1926.

Staff, Frank,
 The Trans-Atlantic Mail, London, 1956.

Stevens, Leonard A.,
 The ELIZABETH: Passage of a QUEEN, New
 York, 1968.

INDEX

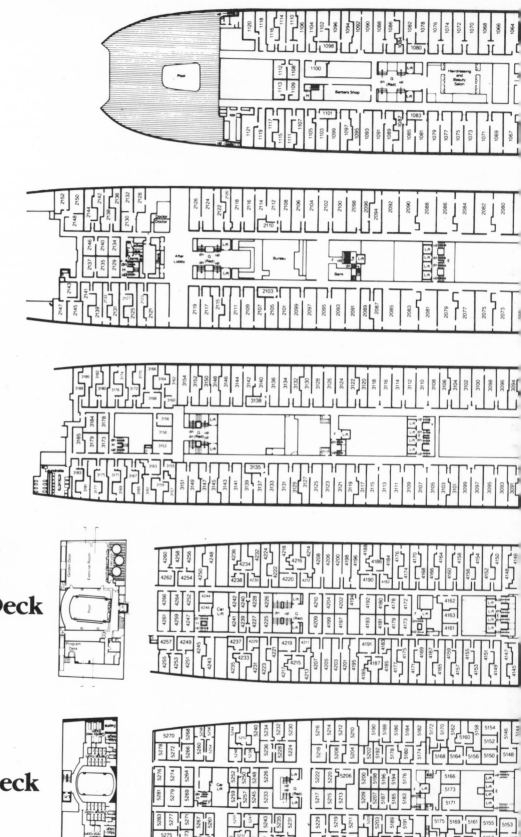

Six Deck

Seven Deck

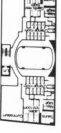